HouseWarmers

Lynda Milligan & Nancy Smith

POSSIBILITIES ®

…Publishers of DreamSpinners® patterns,
I'll Teach Myself® sewing products, and Possibilities® books…

Acknowledgements

We work with a fantastic creative team when we write and design our books. Each one of them is willing to pitch in to do anything and everything, and we value their feedback and hard work. They all help to make work a very fun place to come each day! We would like to take this opportunity to thank each one and to give them a well-deserved pat on the back.

Thank you, Sharon Holmes, for your editing and writing skills and your precise production art. We are grateful to you for making sure all of our "I's" are crossed and our "T's" are dotted. Is that right, Sharon? Our proofreaders keep us on our toes—we thank Chris Scott and Sandi Fruehling for making sure all the pieces and parts fit together.

How did we ever manage without our three excellent artists—Debbe Linn, Valerie Perrone, and Sara Tuttle? Each one of you possesses unique talents and skills that are invaluable! It is so nice to throw out an idea and have it come back better than we could have imagined. Debbe's stippled illustrations fit the theme of HouseWarmers perfectly.

Jane Dumler and Joanne Malone, our fellow designers and stitchers, help make it all fun. They keep us in stitches in every sense of the word. Karlene Coykendall is our top bear maker, and Debbie Andrew pieces with the best of them. It if weren't for Carolyn Schmidt, Sharon Holmes, Jan Hagen, and Marie Gifford, we would just have a lot of tops! They put the quilting in the quilts and the bindings and casings around the edges.

As always, Brian Birlauf did a wonderful job with photography. This time he had the help of our decorating experts, Debbe Linn and Marilyn Robinson, in styling the photos. And we wouldn't have had any houses to warm without the beautiful homes of Aina Martin and Jan Albee. The only problem came when we told them they couldn't keep the quilts!

Thank you, Sara Felton, for your inspired marketing and your clever copy. You always manage to find a new way to say, "Buy this book!" Last, but not least, we thank our Great American Quilt Factory staff for their enthusiasm and the positive comments that keep us on the right track as projects unfold. It has been said that it takes a village to raise a child, but it takes a community of creative friends to produce great books. Thanks everyone!

Lynda & Nancy

Thank you to Hampden Street Antique Market for supplying us with props.
Address: 8964 East Hampden Avenue, Denver, CO 80231. Phone: 303-721-7992.

We enjoy working with fabric lines that we have designed for Peter Pan® Fabrics. The Simply Hearts Quilt uses fabrics from Heart of My Heart and the Flannel Log Cabin is made from Folk Art Flannels. We know that fabric lines come and go, but we are sure that when these lines are gone you will be able to find fabric just as beautiful.

…Publishers of DreamSpinners® patterns,
I'll Teach Myself® sewing products, and Possibilities® books…

HouseWarmers

© 1998 Lynda Milligan & Nancy Smith

Library of Congress Catalog Card Number: 98-065399
ISBN: 1-880972-28-X

Photo Index

Hearthside Homespuns

Block Size: 10″ — 30 blocks

Approximate finished size: 60x70″

Use 42-44″ wide fabric. When strips appear in the cutting list, cut crossgrain strips (selvage to selvage). Purchase extra yardage, if necessary, when substituting half-square triangle methods.

Yardage

Background fabrics (¼ yd. makes 2 blocks)	15 quarter yards
Plaid & homespun fabrics (¼ yd. makes 2 blocks)	15 quarter yards
Border	1¼ yds.
Binding	⅝ yd.
Backing	3⅞ yds.
Batting	66x76″

Cutting

One background (for 2 blocks)	
Corners	4 squares – 3″
Half-square triangle units	*10 squares – 3⅜″
One plaid or homespun (for 2 blocks)	
Center	2 squares – 5½″
Half-square triangle units	*10 squares – 3⅜″
Border	7 strips – 5¼″ wide
Binding	7 strips – 2½″ wide

*Cut these squares in half diagonally to make triangles, or use your favorite method of making half-square triangle units. If using another method, more yardage may be needed.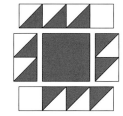

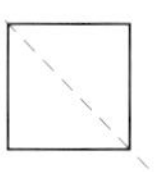

Directions

Use ¼″ seam allowance throughout.

1. Make two blocks from each quarter yard. Make 20 half-square units from the 3⅜″ triangles. Finish blocks by making horizontal rows of units and stitching the rows together.

2. Stitch blocks into six rows of five blocks each.

3. Stitch rows together. Press well.

4. Measure quilt for side borders. Prepare side borders the measured length and stitch to quilt. Repeat for top and bottom borders. Press well.

5. Piece backing horizontally to same size as batting. Use your favorite layering, quilting, and binding meethods to finish quilt.

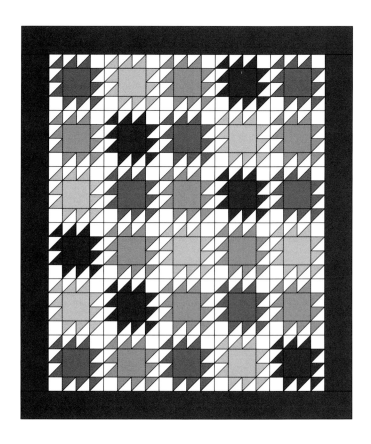

1. 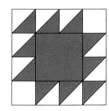 Make 20 (for two blocks)

Hearthside Homespuns Pillowcase

Approximate finished size: 20x30″

Use 42-44″ wide fabric. When strips appear in the cutting list, cut crossgrain strips (selvage to selvage).

Yardage

Main fabric	⅞ yd.
Accent/binding fabric	¼ yd.
Light & dark scraps at least 4″ square	
Backing	1⅜ yds.
Batting	35x44″

Cutting

Main fabric	1 strip – 21″ wide
	1 strip – 3″ wide
Accent fabric	2 strips – 1½″ wide
	1 strip – 2½″ wide
Light triangles for patchwork	*16 squares – 3⅜″
Dark triangles for patchwork	*16 squares – 3⅜″

*Cut these squares in half diagonally
to make triangles.

Directions

Use ¼″ seam allowance unless otherwise noted.

1. Make 32 half-square triangle units with one light and one dark triangle as shown. Stitch into 16 rows of two. Stitch rows together. Press.

2. Measure length of patchwork strip. Trim the 21″, 3″ and 1½″ strips to this length. Stitch the 1½″ strips to both sides of the patchwork. Stitch the 21″ strip to one side and the 3″ strip to the other.

3. Layer with backing and batting. Quilt as desired. Trim raw edges even with top.

4. Fold pillowcase in half, right sides together. Stitch end without patchwork and long side using a ½″ seam allowance.

5. Bind raw edge of pillowcase with the 2½″ strip.

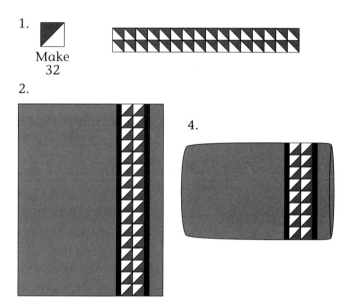

1.

Make 32

2.

4.

5

Cinnamon Stars

Block Size: 6″ — 35 blocks set 5x7 on point

Approximate finished size: 51½x68½″

Use 42-44″ wide fabric. When strips appear in the cutting list, cut crossgrain strips (selvage to selvage). Purchase extra yardage, if necessary, when substituting half-square triangle methods.

Yardage

Background fabric (for blocks, setting squares & triangles, inside border, outside border)	3⅝ yds.
Star fabrics (each ⅛ yd. is for 2 blocks & part of inside pieced border)	18 eighth yards
Binding	½ yd.
Backing	3½ yds.
Batting	57x74″

Cutting

Background fabric (for all blocks)

Block corner squares	140 squares – 2″
Block half-square triangle units	
	*140 squares – 2⅜″
Setting squares	24 squares – 6½″
Setting triangles (sides)	***5 squares – 9¾″
Setting triangles (corners)	**2 squares – 5⅛″
Inside pieced border	*68 squares – 2⅜″
	4 squares – 2″
Outside border	6 strips – 3½″ wide

Star fabrics

Cut the following from each eighth yard for 2 blocks & inside pieced border:

Block center	2 squares – 3½″
Block half-square triangle units	*8 squares – 2⅜″
Inside pieced border	*4 squares – 2⅜″
Binding	6 strips – 2½″ wide

*Cut these squares in half diagonally to make triangles, or use your favorite method of making half-square triangle units (for star point units in blocks and pieced border units). If using another method, more yardage may be needed.

**Cut these two squares in half diagonally to make four triangles.

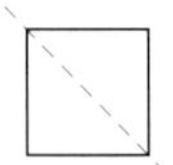

***Cut these five squares in quarters diagonally to make twenty triangles.

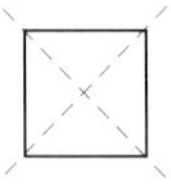

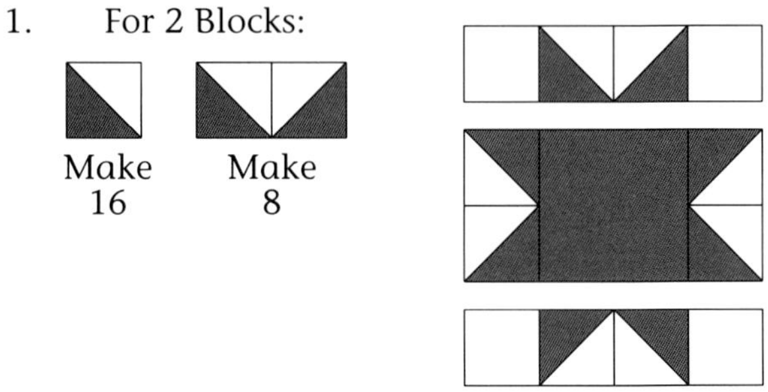

1. For 2 Blocks:

Make 16   Make 8

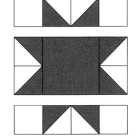

Directions

Use ¼″ seam allowance throughout.

1. Make two blocks from each eighth yard. Make 16 half-square triangle units from the 2⅜″ triangles. For variety in a few blocks, cut the center from a second fabric. Finish blocks by making horizontal rows of units and stitching the rows together.

2. Stitch blocks, setting squares, and setting triangles into diagonal rows as shown.

3. Stitch rows together. Press well.

4. Make 136 half-square triangle units for inside border. Each unit should measure 2″ square. Lay out 40 units for one side border, reversing directions at center as shown in whole-quilt diagram above. Stitch units together with a **scant** ¼″

seam allowance. Press. Lay border edge to edge with quilt center and adjust to fit by making a few seams between units a bit deeper or shallower. Repeat for other side border. Repeat for top and bottom borders using 28 units for each and adding the 2″ background squares at each end.

5. Measure quilt for side borders. Prepare side borders the measured length and stitch to quilt. Repeat for top and bottom borders. Press well.

6. Piece backing horizontally to same size as batting. Use your favorite layering, quilting, and binding methods to finish quilt.

2.

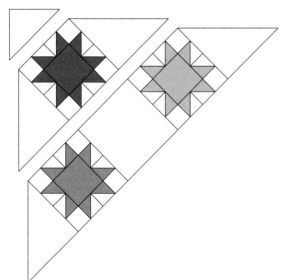

Blue Polar Fleece Blanket

Purchase a lap-size polar fleece blanket. Applique stars, hearts, and bars (cut 1″ wide by various lengths) to edge of blanket. If needed, use a terry towel as a press cloth—do not iron directly on fleece. Star and heart patterns on page 54.

Denim Shirt Throw Pillows

Purchase a large or extra large denim shirt. Remove pockets. Cut shirt open along both side seams. With the front buttons buttoned, cut either a 16½″ or an 18½″ square with the front band centered. Cut a matching square from the shirt back, including some of the yoke, if necessary. Applique stars, hearts, and bars to pillow front as in polar fleece blanket directions above. Embellish with buttons. Place right sides together with backing and stitch around entire outside edge with a ½″ seam allowance. Clip corners, turn through opening (front band). Insert 16″ or 18″ pillow form through opening and button up the front. Star and heart patterns on page 54.

Stars & Bars Dust Ruffle

To a purchased chambray dust ruffle, applique stars, hearts, and bars as in polar fleece blanket directions above. We placed the appliques approximately 2″ from the bottom edge. Stitch large buttons in the gaps between appliques. Star and heart patterns on page 54.

Embellished Sheets & Towels

Topstitch strips of fabric to purchased sheets and towels. Border prints work well for this.

Bittersweet Bear

Made from Bittersweet Bear, DreamSpinners pattern #114. See page 80 for ordering information.

Holiday Stepping Stones

Block Size: 12″ — 17 blocks set on point

Approximate finished size: 70x90″

Use 42-44″ wide fabric. When strips appear in the cutting list, cut crossgrain strips (selvage to selvage).

Yardage

Background (for blocks, sashing strips, setting triangles, & border)	7 yds.
Star points, star appliques	1¾ yds.
"Squares" fabric (for 9-patches, sashing)	⅞ yd.
Vine & leaves	1⅜ yds.
Binding	¾ yd.
Backing	5⅝ yds.
Batting	76x96″

Cutting Patterns on pages 68-69.

Background
Nine-patches	22 strips – 2″ wide
Star centers	17 squares – 3½″
Sashing	44 rectangles – 2½ x 12½″
Star point units	272 squares – 2″
Setting triangles for sides	**2 squares – 21⅛″
Setting triangles for corners	*2 squares – 10″
Border	8 strips – 10½″ wide

Star point/star applique fabric
Star points	136 rectangles – 2x5″
Star appliques	20 stars

"Squares" fabric
Nine-patches	11 strips – 2″ wide
Sashing squares	28 squares – 2½″

Vine/leaf fabric	27″ square
	80 leaves
Binding	9 strips – 2½″ wide

*Cut these two squares in half diagonally to make four triangles.

**Cut these two squares in quarters diagonally to make eight triangles.

Directions

Use ¼″ seam allowance throughout.

MAKE PATCHWORK SECTION OF QUILT

1. Make 68 nine-patch units: Using the 2″ strips of background and 2″ strips of fabric for squares, make seven Strip Set A and four Strip Set B as

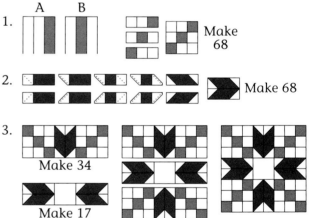

shown. Crosscut into 2″ segments and assemble nine-patch units. See diagram.

2. Make 68 star point units: Place background square for star point unit on end of star point rectangle, right sides together. Mark stitching line with pencil, stitch, and trim, leaving ¼″ seam allowance. Make 68 and 68 reversed. Finish star point units by stitching pairs together. See diagram.

3. Finish piecing 17 blocks as shown.

4. Assemble rows of sashing rectangles and squares. Assemble rows of blocks and sashing rectangles. Diagram on page 9.

5. Stitch one row of sashing to one row of blocks as shown. Stitch sashing to **both** sides of center row. Press well. Diagram on page 9.

6. Stitch setting triangles for sides to ends of rows of blocks (leftover triangles: 2). Diagram on page 69.

7. Stitch rows of blocks/sashing/setting triangles together (leftover triangles: 2). Press well. Staystitch as shown by dotted line. Trim ¼″ outside staystitching. Diagram on page 69.

8. Stitch corner setting triangles to quilt. Square up if necessary. Diagram on page 69. Press.

ADD BORDER & MARK FOR APPLIQUE

1. Measure quilt for side borders. Prepare side borders the measured length and stitch to quilt. Repeat for top and bottom borders.

2. Press quilt top well.

3. Mark a faint line down center of border (5″ from seam). Fold quilt in half lengthwise and mark midpoint of top and bottom borders. Fold in half crosswise and mark midpoint of side borders.

4. Trace one corner vine segment to freezer paper. Make plastic template for side vine segment. Patterns on page 68. Trace 3 side vine segments to freezer paper using template. Trace 4 side vine segments reversed (flip template). Transfer dotted lines to freezer paper. Cut out the 8 freezer paper pieces.

5. Place freezer paper corner segment on quilt top shiny side down, matching dotted lines to drawn line on quilt. Press. Place freezer paper side segments on either side of corner segment, alternating the right-side-up pieces with the reversed pieces. Match ends of freezer paper and dotted lines to marked lines on border. Segments should reach to midpoint mark on top/bottom border and end approximately 1½″ short of midpoint of side border. See diagram with patterns on page 68. Press freezer paper pieces to quilt.

6. Mark placement line along **outside** edge of freezer paper templates. See diagram on page 68. Remove freezer paper, turn quilt one quarter turn, and repeat the process. Repeat for remaining two corners of quilt. Connect the lines at the midpoint of each side border where they did not quite meet.

APPLIQUE BORDER & FINISH QUILT

1. Make stem bias:

   a. From 27″ square, cut bias strips 1⅜″ wide. Stitch ends together diagonally to make 8½ yards (306″).

4.

5.

b. Press bias in half wrong sides together. Do not stretch.

c. Place raw edges of bias strip along placement line on border with folded edge of bias strip toward inside of quilt. Stitch with scant ¼″ seam allowance, making sure folded edge will cover raw edges and placement line when folded over.

d. Applique folded edge down.

2. Applique stars and leaves, using your favorite method, placing as shown in whole-quilt diagram. Press well.

3. Piece backing vertically to same size as batting. Use your favorite layering, quilting, and binding methods to finish quilt.

Throw Pillows – 18″

Use 42-44″ wide fabric. When strips appear in the cutting list, cut crossgrain strips (selvage to selvage).

Yardage

Backing fabric (envelope back)	1¼ yds.
Fabric for optional cording	⅛ yd.
Optional cording (#150 or ⁵⁄₁₆″)	2¼ yds.
Pillow form	18″

Cutting

Fabric for optional cording	2 strips – 1¾″
Backing	2 rectangles – 18½x28″

Directions

1. Using any 12″ or larger block in the book, add borders to make block 18½″ square including seam allowances. If using 19″ block from Good Ole Summertime quilt, cut down to 18½″ square.

2. Optional quilting: Layer with backing and batting squares cut 4″ bigger than top. Quilt in the ditch or as desired. Trim backing and batting to same size as top.

3. Optional cording: Stitch cording strips end to end and cut off to make a strip about 76″ long. Lay cording on wrong side of strip, fold fabric over cording matching raw edges, and stitch semi-close to cording with a zipper foot. Round off pillow top corners slightly. Pin cording to right side of pillow top with raw edges even. To make cording round the corners, clip cording seam allowance 3-4 times no deeper than ⅜″. Trim ends so they overlap ½″. At one end, slide fabric cording cover back and trim off ½″ of cord, then fold raw edge of fabric in ¼″. Wrap folded end around other raw end of cording. Baste cording to pillow top directly on top of previous stitching line.

4. Envelope back: Press the two backing pieces in half, wrong sides together (to 14x18½″). Pin one to right side of pillow top, raw edges even. Pin other backing piece on top of first one, raw edges even, folded edges overlapping in center. Stitch around entire outside edge of pillow with a ½″ seam allowance (if cording was used, stitch as close as possible to cording with zipper foot).

5. Turn right side out. Insert pillow form.

Note: A 15″ Goose in the Pond pillow appears in some photos. Follow above directions, but cut backing rectangles 15½x24″ and use a 15″ pillow form.

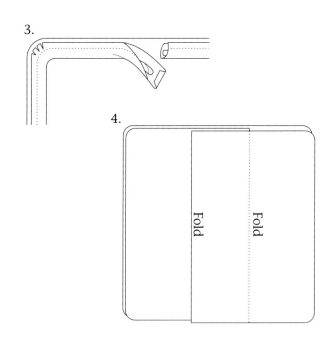

3.

4. Fold Fold

Holiday Stepping Stones Applique Wreath Pillow – 18″

1. Using the diagram and the applique patterns and directions from the Holiday Stepping Stones quilt, page 8, make an 18″ pillow top. Circle for vine is 12″.

2. Finish pillow with the directions at left, including the optional cording.

Green Polar Fleece Blanket

Purchase a lap-size polar fleece blanket. Applique stars in clusters to edge of blanket, placing more in each corner. If needed, use a terry towel as a press cloth—do not iron directly on fleece. Sprinkle large buttons in the gaps between appliques, then stitch in place. Bind the edge of the blanket with 2½″ wide strips of fabric. Star patterns on page 54.

Polar fleece pillowcases are available also and are suitable for embellishing with applique.

Evergreen Mantel Hanging

Block Size: 10″ — 5 blocks set on point

Approximate finished size: 24x71″

Use 42-44″ wide fabric. When strips appear in the cutting list, cut crossgrain strips (selvage to selvage). Purchase extra yardage, if necessary, when substituting half-square triangle methods.

Yardage

Background, backing, binding	3⅝ yds.
Tree fabrics	5 quarter yards
Batting	28x75″

Cutting

Background

Top of mantel hanging	10½x71″
Backing	28x75″
Setting Triangles (top)	***1 square – 15⅜″
Setting Triangles (corners)	**1 square – 8″
Binding	3 strips – 2½″ wide

For all blocks

Squares	10 squares – 2½″
Half-square triangle units	*35 squares – 2⅞″
Large triangle	*3 squares – 6⅞″

Tree fabrics for 1 block

Large triangle (cut first)	*1 square – 6⅞″
Half-square triangle units	*7 squares – 2⅞″
Tree trunk	1 rectangle – 2x5″

*Cut these squares in half diagonally to make triangles, or use your favorite method of making half-square triangle units. If using another method, more yardage may be needed.

**Cut this square in half diagonally to make two triangles.

***Cut this square in quarters diagonally to make four triangles.

Directions

Use ¼″ seam allowance throughout.

1. Make five blocks using directions on page 12. If desired, mix tree fabrics in each block for a scrappy look.

2. Stitch blocks and setting triangles into a row as shown.

3. Stitch 10½x71″ background piece to top of block row. Press well.

4. Layer batting, backing **right** side up, and top **wrong** side up. Pin bottom edge with straight pins.

5. Stitch **bottom edge** only. Trim excess batting and backing away from seam. Carefully clip into seam allowance at Vs between blocks for turning. Turn right side out and press seam well.

6. Baste for quilting. We machine quilted a diagonal grid extending from seamlines in blocks. Trim batting and backing even with top.

7. Bind raw edges at sides and top.

2.

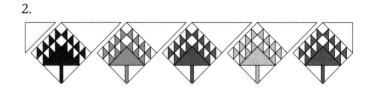

3.

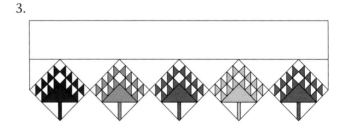

Evergreen

Block Size: 10″ — 12 blocks set on point

Approximate finished size: 56x70″

Use 42-44″ wide fabric. When strips appear in the cutting list, cut crossgrain strips (selvage to selvage). Purchase extra yardage, if necessary, when substituting half-square triangle methods.

Yardage

Background	4¾ yds.
Tree fabrics	12 quarter yards
Binding	⅝ yd.
Backing	3¾ yds.
Batting	62x76″

Cutting

Background

  For all blocks

	Squares	24 squares – 2½″
	Half-square triangle units	*84 squares – 2⅞″
	Large triangle	*6 squares – 6⅞″
Setting Squares		6 squares – 10½″
Setting Triangles (sides)		***3 squares – 15⅜″
Setting Triangles (corners)		**2 squares – 8″
Border – large unit		52 rectangles – 4x7½″
Border – small unit		8 rectangles – 2¼x7½″
Border – corner unit		24 rectangles – 2¼x7½″

Tree fabrics

  For 1 block

	Large triangle (cut first)	*1 square – 6⅞″
	Half-square triangle units	*7 squares – 2⅞″
	Tree trunk	1 rectangle – 2x5″
Border		252 squares (21 of each green) – 2¼″
Binding		7 strips – 2½″ wide

*Cut these squares in half diagonally to make triangles, or use your favorite method of making half-square triangle units. If using another method, more yardage may be needed.

**Cut these two squares in half diagonally to make four triangles.

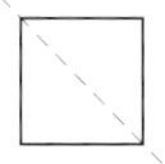

***Cut these three squares in quarters diagonally to make twelve triangles.

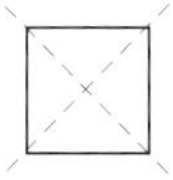

1.

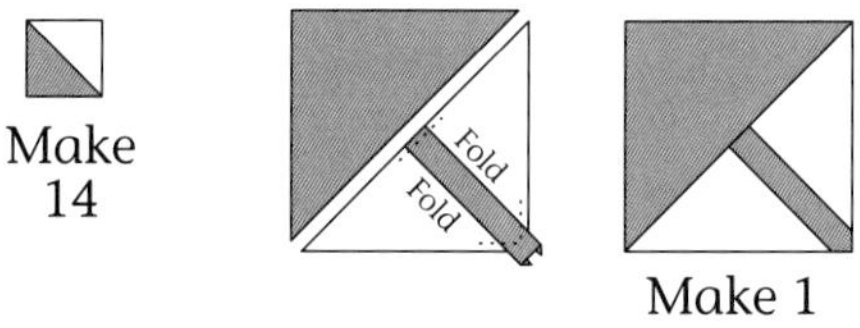

Make 14

Make 1

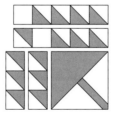 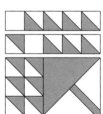 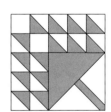

Directions

Use ¼″ seam allowance throughout.

1. For one block:

  a. Make 14 half-square triangle units using 2⅞″ triangles.

  b. Press ¼″ seam allowance to wrong side on each long side of tree trunk piece.

  c. Place wrong side of tree trunk to right side of large background triangle, centering as shown. Baste ends of trunk in place.

d. Stitch large dark triangle to large background triangle, right sides together, catching tree trunk in seam. Trim excess seam allowance of trunk at corner.

e. Finish block as shown.

f. Applique edges of trunks.

2. Make 11 more blocks.

3. Stitch blocks, setting squares, and setting triangles into diagonal rows as shown.

4. Stitch rows together. Press well.

5. Border:

a. Large Unit: Place dark square right sides together on background rectangle, mark stitching line with pencil, stitch, and trim to ¼" seam allowance. See diagram. Make 52 units with triangles added to all four corners.

b. Small Unit: Make 8 as above with triangles at both ends. See diagram.

c. Corner Units:

1. Make 12 as above with one triangle only. Make 12 reversed. Stitch into sets of three. See diagram.

2. Pin two reverse-image sets right sides together, matching seams, and stitch diagonal seam from raw edge at corner to raw edge at other side, stitching through seam intersection where green triangles meet. See diagrams. Trim excess as shown. Set in corner square. Press well. Repeat for other three corner units.

d. Make two side borders with 15 large units and two small units as shown. Use **scant** ¼" seam allowances. Press well. Lay edge to edge with quilt center and adjust to fit by making a few seams between units a bit deeper or shallower. Stitch to quilt.

e. Make top and bottom borders with 11 large and two small units plus two corner units. See diagram. Press well and adjust to fit as above. Stitch to quilt. Press well.

6. Piece backing horizontally to same size as batting. Use your favorite layering, quilting, and binding methods to finish quilt. Quilting pattern on page 65.

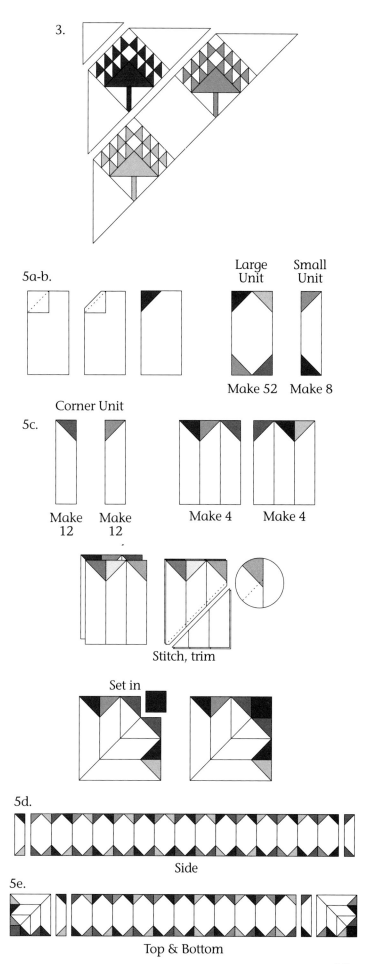

3.

5a-b.

Large Unit   Small Unit

Make 52   Make 8

Corner Unit

5c.

Make 12   Make 12   Make 4   Make 4

Stitch, trim

Set in

5d.

Side

5e.

Top & Bottom

Autumn Leaves

Block size: 6″ — 83 blocks set on point

Approximate finished size: 42½x59½″

Use 42-44″ wide fabric. When strips appear in the cutting list, cut crossgrain strips (selvage to selvage). Purchase extra yardage, if necessary, when substituting half-square triangle methods.

Yardage

Background fabrics (⅛ yd. makes 2 blocks)	42 eighth yards
Leaf fabrics (⅛ yd. makes 2 blocks)	42 eighth yards
Binding	½ yd.
Backing	3 yds.
Batting	49x66″

Cutting

Background fabric (for 2 blocks)	2 squares – 2½″
	*4 squares – 2⅞″
	4 rectangles – 2¼x4″
Leaf fabric (for 2 blocks)	6 squares – 2½″
	*4 squares – 2⅞″
	2 rectangles – 1x4″
Binding	6 strips – 2½″ wide

*Cut these squares in half diagonally to make triangles, or use your favorite method of making half-square triangle units. If using another method, more yardage may be needed.

Directions

Use ¼″ seam allowance throughout.

1. Make eight half-square triangle units from the 2⅞″ triangles.

2. Make stem units:

   a. Make 83 copies of Paper Piecing Pattern for Stem Unit, page 15.

   b. Center 1x4″ rectangle of leaf fabric **right** side up on **wrong** side of paper piecing pattern over stem area. Make two units with each leaf fabric.

   c. Lay 2¼x4″ rectangle of background fabric **right** sides and raw edges together on leaf fabric. Stitch on line on **right** side of paper pattern. Press open.

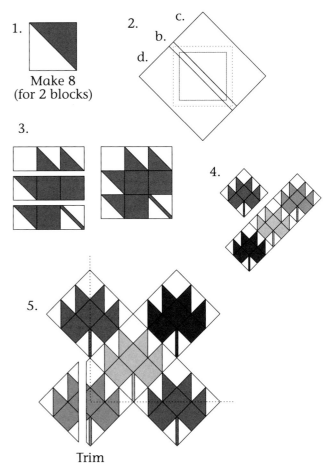

1. Make 8 (for 2 blocks)

2. c. b. d.

3.

4.

5.

Trim

d. Repeat with another rectangle of background fabric on other side of stem unit. Press open.

e. Trim along dotted line. Tear off paper.

3. Finish blocks by making horizontal rows of units and stitching the rows together.

4. Stitch blocks into diagonal rows as shown.

5. Stitch diagonal rows together. Staystitch through centers of outer blocks as shown. Trim ¼" outside staystitching.

6. Piece backing horizontally to same size as batting. Use your favorite layering, quilting, and binding methods to finish quilt.

Autumn Leaves

Paper Piecing Pattern for Stem Unit

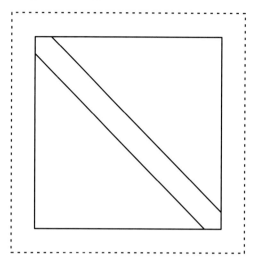

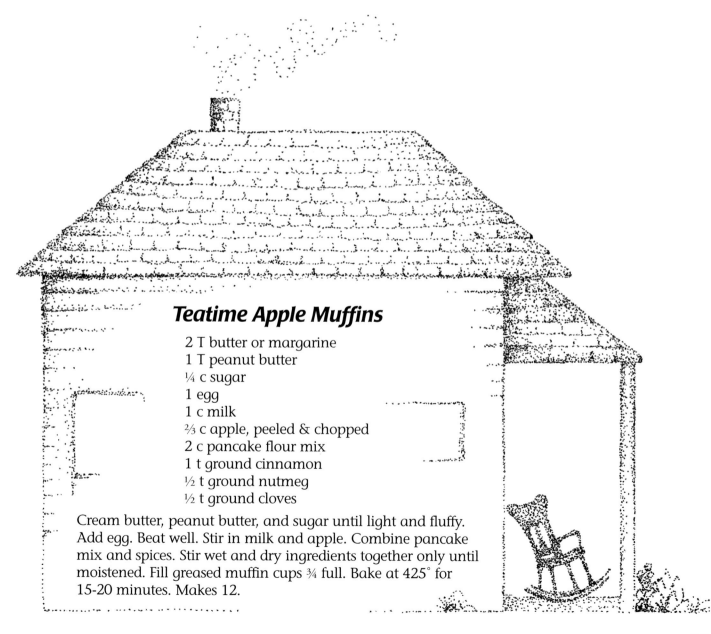

Teatime Apple Muffins

2 T butter or margarine
1 T peanut butter
¼ c sugar
1 egg
1 c milk
⅔ c apple, peeled & chopped
2 c pancake flour mix
1 t ground cinnamon
½ t ground nutmeg
½ t ground cloves

Cream butter, peanut butter, and sugar until light and fluffy. Add egg. Beat well. Stir in milk and apple. Combine pancake mix and spices. Stir wet and dry ingredients together only until moistened. Fill greased muffin cups ¾ full. Bake at 425° for 15-20 minutes. Makes 12.

Still Life

Block size: 20″

Approximate finished size: 31″ square

Use 42-44″ wide fabric. When strips appear in the cutting list, cut crossgrain strips (selvage to selvage).

Yardage

Background, Border 1 (dark)	¾ yd.
Applique fabrics	scraps up to 8x13″
Borders 1 & 2 (light)	¾ yd.
Binding	⅜ yd.
Backing	1⅛ yds.
Batting	35x35″

Cutting Patterns on pages 72-79.

Background, Border 1 (dark)	1 square – 20½″
	**4 squares – 6¼″
Applique fabrics	1 from each pattern
Borders 1 & 2 (light)	*2 squares – 5⅞″
	**3 squares – 6¼″
	4 strips – 3½″ wide
Binding	4 strips – 2½″ wide

*Cut these squares in half diagonally to make triangles.

**Cut these squares in quarters diagonally to make triangles.

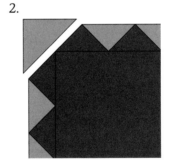

Make 4

Directions

Use ¼″ seam allowance throughout.

1. Make four Border 1 strips as shown with 6¼″ triangles, then stitch to sides of center background square.

2. Stitch 5⅞″ triangles to corners of quilt. Press well.

3. Measure length of quilt and cut side borders that measurement. Stitch to sides of quilt.

4. Measure width of quilt and cut top and bottom borders that measurement. Stitch to top and bottom of quilt. Press.

5. Applique fruit, using your favorite method, placing as shown in diagram.

6. Use your favorite layering, quilting, and binding methods to finish quilt. We quilted and then framed the one in the photo.

Autumn Leaves & Still Life 17

Trip Around the World

Unit Size: 2″

Approximate finished size: 53½″ square

Use 42-44″ wide fabric. When strips appear in the cutting list, cut crossgrain strips (selvage to selvage).

Yardage

Fabrics for strip sets

E, F	¼ yd. each
A, G, H, I	⅜ yd. each
B, C	½ yd. each
D	⅝ yd.
Border 1	⅞ yd.
Border 2	½ yd.
Binding	½ yd.
Backing	3½ yds.
Batting	58x58″

Cutting

Fabrics for strip sets	
E, F	2 strips each – 2½″ wide
A, G, H, I	4 strips each – 2½″ wide
B, C	6 strips each – 2½″ wide
D	7 strips – 2½″ wide
H	1 square – 2½″
Border 1	5 strips – 4½″ wide
Border 2	6 strips – 2¼″ wide
Binding	6 strips – 2½″ wide

Directions

Use ¼″ seam allowance throughout.

1. Cut strips for strip sets into thirds, approximately 14″ long each (strips are now 2½x14″). Make piles of strips of each fabric and label them with their letter name.

2. Make one each of the 11 strip sets shown using the 14″ strips. Label the strip sets as they are made. Press seams of odd-numbered strip sets to right and seams of even-numbered strip sets to left. Leave Strip Set 11 unpressed.

3. Crosscut strip sets into four 2½″ segments.

4. Lay out segments for one quarter of quilt as shown. Stitch together. Repeat for other three quarters.

5. Lay out quilt, rotating the four quarters as shown. Lay Strip Set 11 segments between the

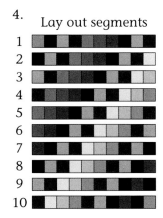

2. Strip Sets

1 A B C D E F G B C D
2 B C D E F G B C D H
3 C D E F G B C D H I
4 D E F G B C D H I A
5 E F G B C D H I A D

6 F G B C D H I A D C
7 G B C D H I A D C B
8 B C D H I A D C B G
9 C D H I A D C B G B
10 D H I A D C B G B A

11 H I A D C B G B A I

3. Crosscut

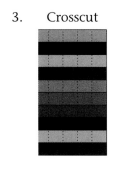

4. Lay out segments

1
2
3
4
5
6
7
8
9
10

quarters, rotating as shown. Place the 2½″ square of Fabric H in the center. Stitch parts into horizontal rows, then stitch the rows together. Press.

6. Border 1: Measure quilt for side borders. Prepare side borders the measured length and stitch to quilt. Repeat for top and bottom borders.

7. Border 2: Repeat Step 6. Press well.

8. Piece backing to same size as batting. Use your favorite layering, quilting, and binding methods to finish quilt. Quilting pattern on page 51.

5.

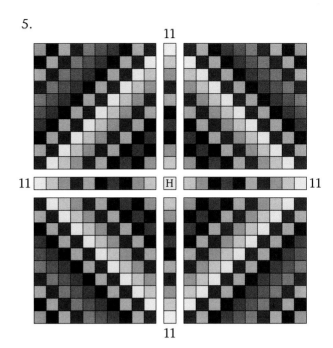

4. Make 4

Heart in Hand Cookies

2 c sugar   ½ t baking soda
1 pound butter   1 t salt
3 eggs   2-3 t vanilla
1 t baking powder   6 c flour

Cream butter and sugar until light and fluffy. Add eggs and vanilla. Beat well. Combine dry ingredients. Combine butter mixture and dry ingredients. Chill 1 hour. Roll out to ¼″ thickness. Cut with heart-in-hand cookie cutter. Bake at 350° for 8-10 minutes.

19

Garden Wall Hanging

Unit Size: 2″

Approximate finished size: 36″ square

Use 42-44″ wide fabric. When strips appear in the cutting list, cut crossgrain strips (selvage to selvage).

Yardage

Fabrics for strip sets

A	⅔ yd.
B, C, E, F	⅓ yd. each
D	¼ yd.
Fabrics for appliques (A-F or 6 total)	¼ yd. each
Border	½ yd.
Binding	⅜ yd.
Backing	1¼ yds.
Batting	40x40″

Cutting Patterns on pages 62-63.

Fabrics for strip sets	A – 8 strips – 2½″ wide
	B, C, E, F – 3 strips each – 2½″ wide
	D – 2 strips – 2½″ wide
	A – 1 square – 2½″
Fabrics for appliques	as desired – see diagram
Border	4 strips – 3½″ wide
Binding	4 strips – 2½″ wide

Directions

Use ¼″ seam allowance throughout.

1. Cut strips for strip sets into thirds, approximately 14″ long each (strips are now 2½x14″). Make piles of strips of each fabric and label them with their letter name.

2. Make one each of the 8 strip sets shown using the 14″ strips. Label the strip sets as they are made. Press seams of odd-numbered strip sets to right and seams of even-numbered strip sets to left. Leave Strip Set 8 unpressed.

3. Crosscut strip sets into four 2½″ segments.

4. Lay out segments for one quarter of quilt as shown. Stitch together. Repeat for other three quarters.

5. Lay out quilt, rotating the four quarters as shown. Lay Strip Set 8 segments between the quarters, rotating as shown, and the 2½″ square of Fabric A in the center. Stitch parts into horizontal rows, then stitch the rows together. Press.

22

2. Strip Sets

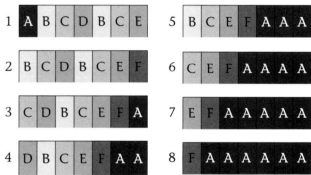

3. Crosscut   4. Lay out segments

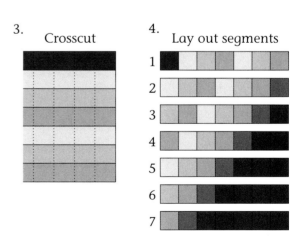

6. Border: Measure quilt for side borders. Cut side borders the measured length and stitch to quilt. Repeat for top and bottom borders. Press well.

7. Applique center of quilt with your favorite method, placing as shown in diagram. Patterns must be reversed in some cases to duplicate our layout. One large, two medium, and two small leaf patterns are given to be used as desired.

8. Use your favorite layering, quilting, and binding methods to finish quilt.

4.
Make 4

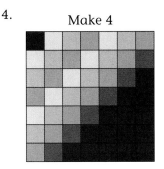

5.

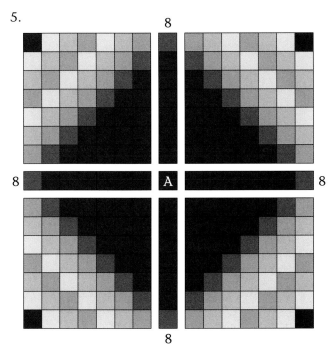

Garden Chairbacks

Garden Chairbacks

Size: 12x15″

Yardage for four

Center	⅜ yd.
Appliques	scraps up to 7x8″ or quarter yards
Border 1	¼ yd.
Border 2	½ yd.
Binding	½ yd.
Backing	1⅛ yds.
Ties	1¼ yds.
Batting	4 rectangles – 16x19″

Cutting for four. Patterns on pages 62-63.

Center	4 rectangles – 7½x10½″
Applique fabrics	use as desired
Border 1	4 strips – 1½″ wide
Border 2	6 strips – 2″ wide
Binding	6 strips – 2½″ wide
Backing	4 rectangles – 16x19″
Ties	16 strips – 2½x30″

Directions

Use ¼″ seam allowance throughout.

1. Borders 1 & 2: Stitch strips to sides of center rectangle and then top and bottom, trimming off remaining ends of strips after stitching. Press.

2. Applique block with your favorite method, referring to photos and diagrams at left for placement.

3. Make small quilts by layering, quilting, and binding with your favorite methods.

4. Ties: Fold each strip lengthwise, right sides together. Stitch, leaving a 4″ opening at center of long side. Turn, press. Slipstitch opening closed. Hold quilted block up to chair and mark best position for ties with pins. Pin ties on back of block as shown in diagram. Stitch in ditch from right side.

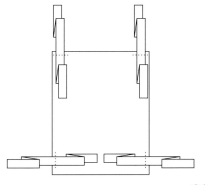

24 Cinnamon Stars & Hearthside Homespuns

Starry Night

Block Size: 6″ — 9 blocks set 3 x 3 with sashing

Approximate finished size: 34″ square

Use 42-44″ wide fabric. When strips appear in the cutting list, cut crossgrain strips (selvage to selvage).

Yardage

Background (for blocks, sashing strips, & border)	1¾ yds.
Trees	9 scraps at least 8″ square
Tree trunks	⅛ yd.
Stars	⅜ yd.
Binding	⅜ yd.
Backing	1⅛ yds.
Batting	40x40″

Cutting Patterns on page 67.

Background	
Pattern C & Pattern C Reversed	9 each
Piece D	18 rectangles – 2x 2¾″
Piece E	36 rectangles – 2½ x 6½″
Piece F	20 squares – 2½″
Border	4 strips – 2½″ wide
Tree – Pattern A	9
Tree trunk – Piece B	9 squares – 2″
Star	
Piece G	16 squares – 2½″
Piece H	128 squares – 1½″
Binding	4 strips – 2½″ wide

Directions

Use ¼″ seam allowance throughout.

1. Piece 9 tree blocks as shown (A, B, C, & D).

2. Piece 24 sashing rectangles. Lay H on corner of E right sides together, mark stitching line with pencil, stitch, and trim, leaving a ¼″ seam allowance. Repeat on remaining three corners.

3. Piece 16 sashing squares (F & H) as shown, using the method in Step 2.

4. Assemble 3 tree rows.

5. Assemble 4 sashing rows.

6. Assemble the 2 extra sashing rows for top and bottom of quilt.

7. Stitch tree and sashing rows together. Press well.

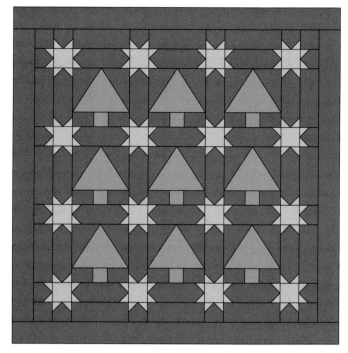

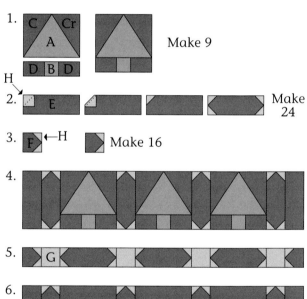

8. Measure quilt for side borders. Cut side borders the measured length and stitch to quilt. Repeat for top and bottom borders. Press well.

9. Use your favorite layering, quilting, and binding methods to finish quilt.

Starry Night Chairbacks

Size: 14x18″

Yardage for four

Center	¾ yd.
Appliques	scraps up to 5x7″ or quarter yards
Border	⅝ yd.
Binding	⅔ yd.
Backing	1⅜ yds.
Ties	⅔ yd.
Batting	4 rectangles – 17x21″

Cutting for four. Patterns on page 59.

Center	4 rectangles – 11x15″
Applique fabrics	use as desired
Border	8 strips – 2″ wide
Binding	8 strips – 2½″ wide
Backing	4 rectangles – 17x21″
Ties	8 strips – 2½x30″

Directions

Use ¼″ seam allowance throughout.

1. Border: Stitch strips to sides of center rectangle and then top and bottom, trimming off remaining ends of strips after stitching. Press.

2. Make a 125% copy of the patterns. Applique block with your favorite method, referring to photos and diagrams for placement.

3. Make small quilts by layering, quilting, and binding with your favorite methods.

4. Ties: Fold each strip lengthwise, right sides together. Stitch, leaving a 4″ opening at center of long side. Turn, press. Slipstitch opening closed. Hold quilted block up to chair and mark best position for ties with pins. Pin ties on back of block as shown in diagram. Stitch in ditch from right side.

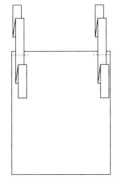

Starry Night Hot Pad

Size: 8½″ square

Yardage

Background/pocket	¼ yd.
Appliques	scraps up to 5x6″ or sixth yards
Cotton batting	2 squares – 9″

Cutting Patterns on page 59.

Background/pocket	2 squares – 9″
	1 rectangle – 9x12″
Applique fabrics	use as desired

Directions

Use ¼″ seam allowance throughout.

1. Fold fabric rectangle in half wrong sides together to make a 9x6″ rectangle for pocket.

2. Applique design on pocket (place fold at left).

3. Pin appliqued rectangle to right side of one 9″ square of fabric, raw edges even. Applique star to upper left corner.

4. Layer batting squares, remaining 9″ fabric square right side up, appliqued square right side down.

5. Stitch around outside edge, leaving 4″ open on one side for turning. Trim corners, turn, press. Whipstitch opening closed. Topstitch ¼″ from edge.

6. Stitch buttons through all layers near folded edge, one placed 2½″ from top and one 4½″ from top. The pocket formed at the bottom holds 3x5″ recipe cards.

Place Mats & Napkins

Applique Starry Night house/tree to purchased place mats and larger tree with star to purchased napkins. Patterns on page 59.

28   Toasty Triangles & Flannel Log Cabin

Path Through the Pines

Block Size: 12″ — 17 tree blocks, 22 star blocks

Approximate finished size: 84x108″

Use 42-44″ wide fabric. When strips appear in the cutting list, cut crossgrain strips (selvage to selvage).

Yardage

Background	5 yds.
Trees	1¾ yds.
Tree trunks	¼ yd.
Stars	2½ yds.
"Squares" fabric for 4-patches	1 yd.
Border	3 yds.
Binding	⅞ yd.
Backing	7¾ yds.
Batting	90x114″

Cutting Patterns on pages 70-71.

Background
Patterns A, B, C	17 each
Patterns A, B, C reversed	17 each
For trunk unit	4 strips – 5¾″ wide
Pattern G for star point unit	88
For 4-patch unit	11 strips – 2½″ wide

Tree fabric
Patterns D, E, F	17 each

Trunk fabric	2 strips – 2″ wide

Star fabric
Center squares	22 squares – 4½″
Pattern H & pattern H reversed	88 each

"Squares" fabric for 4-patches	11 strips – 2½″ wide
Border	8 strips – 12½″ wide
Binding	10 strips – 2½″ wide

Directions

Use ¼″ seam allowance throughout.

1. Make tree block:

   a. Make two strip sets for the trunk unit by sewing one trunk strip between two background strips. Press. Crosscut into 17 segments 3½″ wide.

   b. Make top three tree units of tree blocks as shown.

   c. Assemble 17 blocks by stitching the four units together.

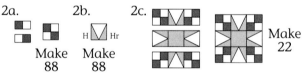

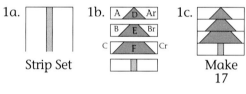

1a. Strip Set

1b.

1c. Make 17

2a. 2b. Make 88 / Make 88 2c. Make 22

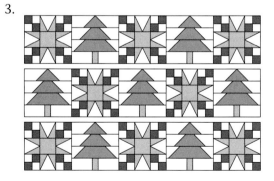

3.

2. Make star block:

   a. Make 11 strip sets for the four-patch unit by sewing a 2½″ background strip to a 2½″ "squares" fabric strip. Press. Crosscut into 176 segments 2½″ wide. Stitch two segments together as shown. Make 88 four-patch units.

b. Make 88 star point units as shown.

c. Assemble units into 22 blocks as shown.

3. Alternating blocks, stitch blocks into seven rows of five. See diagram.

4. Stitch rows together. Press well.

5. Measure width and length of quilt center. Prepare side borders the measured length and stitch to quilt. Prepare top and bottom borders the measured length, then stitch remaining star blocks to both ends of each. Stitch top and bottom borders to quilt. Press well.

6. Piece backing horizontally to same size as batting. Use your favorite layering, quilting, and binding methods to finish quilt.

Path Through the Pines Valance

Height: 17″ – width is adjustable – use 2½″ rod

Use 42-44″ wide fabric. When strips appear in the cutting list, cut crossgrain strips (selvage to selvage).

For best results, heading/lining fabric should be the same fabric as the block background.

Figure number of blocks to make: Measure window width and multiply by two. Divide answer by twelve and round up to nearest number.

Example: Window width = 71″
             71″ x 2 = 142″
             142″ ÷ 12 = 11.8″
             Round up to 12 blocks

Figure block yardage: Each tree block takes ⅛ yard each of green and light brown and a 2x3½″ piece of dark brown. Figure yardage needed according to how many tree blocks are needed. For example, 12 tree blocks would take 1½ yards of green and ⅙ yard of dark brown. The light brown block background yardage is included below in the heading/lining yardage.

Figure heading/lining yardage: The full width of the valance will be needed. For example, for twelve tree blocks: 12 blocks x 12″ = 144″ = 4 yards + ¼ yard for shrinkage and seam allowances = 4¼ yards. Cut off a piece 24″ x the length of the fabric for the heading/lining and set it aside, then use the other long narrow piece of fabric for cutting out the background for the blocks.

Directions

Use ¼″ seam allowance throughout.

1. Make tree blocks using directions on page 30. There would be considerable waste if making two strip sets for the trunk units, so it is advis-able to cut trunks 2x3½″ and background pieces for each side of trunk 5¾x3½″, and piece each tree trunk unit individually.

2. Stitch blocks together in a row. Press.

3. Measure the width of the row of blocks. Cut a piece of heading/lining fabric this length by 22½″.

4. Stitch one long side of heading/lining to bottom of block row, right sides together. Stitch other side to top of block row, right sides together, forming a tube.

5. Press and then stitch ¼″ hem to wrong side on both open ends.

6. Press valance in half with bottom edge of tree blocks as one edge.

7. Casing: Measure up 3″ from seam at top of tree blocks and draw a line the full width of the valance. Stitch on mark and in the seam at the top of the tree blocks.

4.

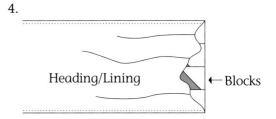

Heading/Lining   ← Blocks

7.

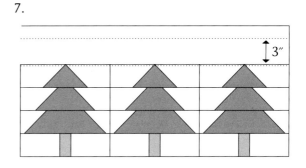

3″

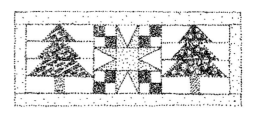

31

32 Path Through the Pines

Friendship Pillows

Approximate size: 10x11″

These sweet little pillows were made with scraps and imagination. No yardage given.

Cutting Patterns on pages 54, 55, 58.

Background	6½x7½″
Borders	8 rectangles – 1½x12″
Backing	10½x11½″

Directions

Use ¼″ seam allowance throughout.

1. Borders 1 & 2: Stitch strips to sides of block and then top and bottom, trimming off remaining ends of strips after stitching. Press.

2. Make a 120% copy of the pattern. Applique block with your favorite method. Trace lettering and other details to block with permanent marking pen, or embroider.

3. Optional: Embellish with buttons sewn on with six strands of embroidery floss.

4. Pin pillow top to backing right sides together. Stitch around edge, leaving 4″ opening for stuffing. Trim corners, turn, stuff. Slipstitch opening closed.

Friendship Wall Hangings

Approximate size: 15x17″

These sweet little wall hangings were made with scraps and imagination. No yardage given.

Use 42-44″ wide fabric. When strips appear in the cutting list, cut crossgrain strips (selvage to selvage).

Cutting Patterns on pages 54, 55, 58.

Background	7½x9½″
Border 1	4 rectangles – 1½x12″
Border 2	4 rectangles – 3½x18″
Binding	2 strips – 2½″ wide
Backing	17x19″

Directions

Use ¼″ seam allowance throughout.

1. Borders 1 & 2: Stitch strips to sides of block and then top and bottom, trimming off remaining ends of strips after stitching. Press.

2. Make a 140% copy of the pattern. Applique block with your favorite method. Trace lettering and other details to block with permanent marking pen, or embroider.

3. Optional: Embellish with buttons sewn on with six strands of embroidery floss.

4. Use your favorite layering, quilting, and binding methods to finish wall hanging.

Toasty Triangles

Unit Size: 5″ — 287 units set on point

Approximate finished size: 77x91″

Use 42-44″ wide fabric. When strips appear in the cutting list, cut crossgrain strips (selvage to selvage). Purchase extra yardage, if necessary, when substituting half-square triangle methods.

Yardage

Light & medium-light scraps at least 7″ square	to total 4⅜ yds.
Dark & medium-dark scraps at least 7″ square	to total 4⅜ yds.
Binding	¾ yd.
Backing	7¼ yds.
Batting	83x97″

Cutting

Lights/medium-lights	*150 squares – 5⅞″
Darks/medium-darks	*150 squares – 5⅞″
Binding	9 strips – 2½″ wide

*Cut these squares in half diagonally to make triangles, or use your favorite method of making half-square triangle units. If using another method, more yardage may be needed.

Directions

Use ¼″ seam allowance throughout.

1. Make 287 half-square triangle units as shown. There should be 12 light triangles and 12 dark triangles left to use for setting triangles at the top and bottom of the quilt.

2. Stitch units into rows as shown. Light setting triangles finish the top of the first 12 rows, and dark triangles finish the bottom of the last 12 rows.

3. Stitch diagonal rows together.

4. Staystitch sides as shown. Trim ¼″ outside staystitching. Press well.

5. Piece backing horizontally to same size as batting. Use your favorite layering, quilting, and binding methods to finish quilt.

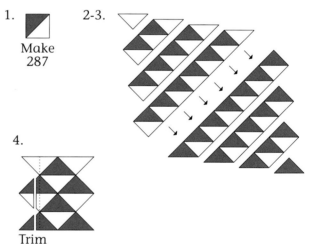

1.
Make 287

2-3.

4.
Trim

Flannel Log Cabin

Block Size: 19″ — 12 blocks

Approximate finished size: 57x76″

Use 42-44″ wide fabric. When strips appear in the cutting list, cut crossgrain strips (selvage to selvage).

Yardage

Log/center fabrics

Color 1 (one side of one block)	3 eighth yards
Color 2 (one side of one block)	3 eighth yards
Color 3 (one side of five blocks)	5 quarter yards
Color 4 (one side of five blocks)	5 quarter yards
Color 5 (one side of all blocks)	5 half yards

Binding	⅝ yd.
Backing	3¾ yds.
Batting	63x82″

Cutting

Centers

Color 1	1 square – 3½″
Color 2	1 square – 3½″
Color 3	5 squares – 3½″
Color 4	5 squares – 3½″

Log fabrics

Color 1	3 strips – 2½″
Color 2	3 strips – 2½″
Color 3	15 strips – 2½″
Color 4	15 strips – 2½″
Color 5	30 strips – 2½″

Binding	7 strips – 2½″ wide

Directions

Use ¼″ seam allowance throughout.

1. Make 12 blocks by stitching strips to center squares in four clockwise rounds. After stitching each strip to block, trim off remaining end of strip. See diagram. Press.

   a. One block: Color 1 for the center and the third and fourth logs of each round. Color 5 for the first and second logs of each round.

   b. One block: Same as block above, substituting Color 2 for Color 1. Color 5 is the same.

   c. Five blocks: Same as blocks above, substituting Color 3 for Color 1. Color 5 is the same.

   d. Five blocks: Same as blocks above, substituting Color 4 for Color 1. Color 5 is the same.

2. Lay out blocks, rotating as needed to match diagram. Stitch into four rows of three blocks.

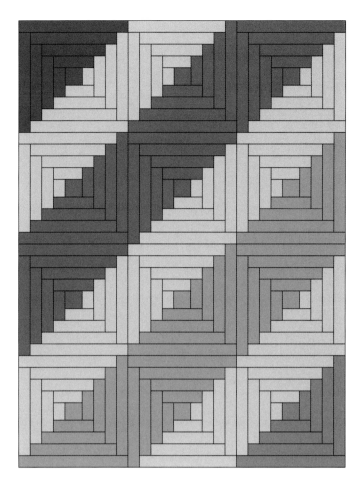

Round 1

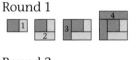

Round 2

Round 3

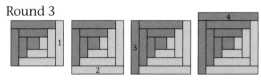

Round 4

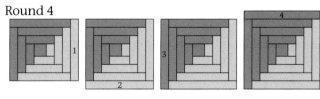

3. Stitch rows together. Press well.

4. Piece backing horizontally to same size as batting. Use your favorite layering, quilting, and binding methods to finish quilt.

35

Simply Hearts

"Block" Size: 7½" — 20 "blocks"

Approximate finished size: 52x59½"

Use 42-44″ wide fabric. When strips appear in the cutting list, cut crossgrain strips (selvage to selvage).

We used a border print for Border 2. Yardage for borders will vary when border prints are substituted.

Yardage

Background, borders 2 & 4	2⅝ yds.
Borders 1 & 3	⅜ yd.
Hearts – scraps at least 7″ square	20
Binding	½ yd.
Backing	3½ yds.
Batting	58x66″

Cutting Pattern on page 37.

Background	
Center panel	38½x46″
Border 2	5 strips – 2½″ wide
Border 4	6 strips – 4½″ wide
Borders 1 & 3	10 strips – 1″ wide
Hearts	20
Binding	6 strips – 2½″ wide

Directions

Use ¼″ seam allowance throughout.

1. Mark center panel lightly with a pencil: First mark a line 4¼″ in from all raw edges, avoiding marking in the corners. Then divide the rectangle into four parts across and five down and mark the corresponding verticals and horizontals. The resulting squares should be 7½″.

2. Applique a heart in the center of each marked square, using your favorite method. Press lightly.

3. Border 1: Measure quilt for side borders. Prepare side borders the measured length and stitch to quilt. Repeat for top and bottom. Press.

4. Borders 2-4: Repeat Step 3. Press borders well.

5. Piece backing horizontally to same size as batting. Use your favorite layering, quilting, and binding methods to finish quilt.

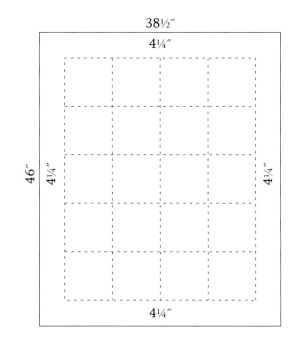

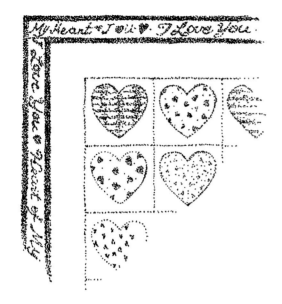

White Polar Fleece Blanket

Purchase a bed-size polar fleece blanket. Cut out strips of a border print and topstitch to blanket approximately 3″ in from edge. Depending on the border print, the corners can cross over each other, or they can be mitered simply by folding under a 45° angle before topstitching.

Simply Hearts

Pineapple

Block Size: 17″ — 12 blocks

Approximate finished size: 51x68″

Use 42-44″ wide fabric. When strips appear in the cutting list, cut crossgrain strips (selvage to selvage).

The directions for this quilt require the use of the Pineapple Rule, available by mail from Possibilities®. See page 80.

Yardage

Center square	⅓ yd.
Log fabrics	30-35 quarter yards
Binding	⅝ yd.
Backing	3½ yds.
Batting	57x74″

Cutting

Centers	12 squares – 4″
Logs	80-85 strips – 2½″ wide
Round 8 (corners)	10 strips – 3″ wide
Binding	7 strips – 2½″ wide

General Directions

Use ¼″ seam allowance throughout.

1. Make 12 blocks. Press.
2. Stitch into four rows of three blocks.
3. Stitch rows together. Press well.
4. Piece backing horizontally to same size as batting. Use your favorite layering, quilting, and binding methods to finish quilt.

Directions For One Block

ROUND 1: Mark diagonal lines from corner to corner across wrong side of center square. Cut four 4″ segments from the 2½″ strips cut for logs (use four different fabrics). Stitch to opposite sides of center square. Stitch others to remaining sides. Carefully press seam allowances toward outside of block; do not stretch square out of shape.

Order of Rounds

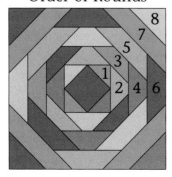

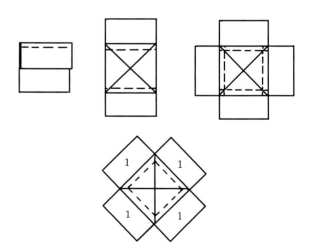

Lay Pineapple Rule on wrong side of block, **inside diagonal lines on ruler on top of seamline and center vertical line matching marked center line on center square.** A horizontal line on ruler may not fall exactly on the horizontal pencil line but should be parallel and equidistant from it. Trim off the two triangles of fabric at corner. Repeat at other corners of block.

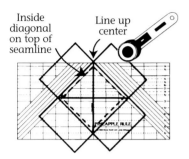

Inside diagonal on top of seamline

Line up center

ROUND 2: Cut four 5½″ segments (different fabrics) and stitch to block as in Round 1. They will be slightly longer than necessary. Press seam allowances to outside of block. Draw lines from corner to corner, keeping right angle at center. Lay ruler on block as before, **lining up the inside diagonal lines on the seamline.** Trim corners.

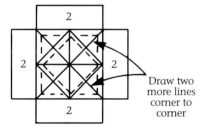

Draw two more lines corner to corner

Trim two triangles at each corner

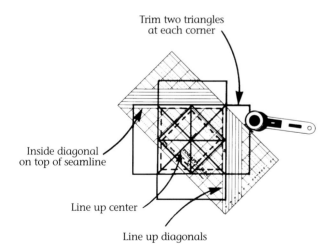

Inside diagonal on top of seamline

Line up center

Line up diagonals

ROUND 3: Cut four 7″ segments (different fabrics) and stitch to block. Press, being careful not to stretch the block. Trim the corners, **this time lining up the edge of the ruler with the edge of Round 2.** Continue to use center, horizontal, and diagonal guidelines on ruler.

HINT
Try to use the same horizontal guide for each side of every block.

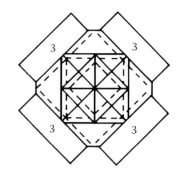

Line up edge of ruler with edge of Round 2

Line up center

Line up diagonals

Line up horizontals

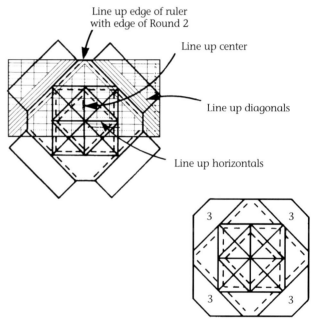

CONTINUED ON PAGE 48

HINT
To follow all guides, you may need to trim or extend an edge. For example, you may have to move the ruler up or down, away from the edge of the previous round, in order to match the guidelines. This inaccuracy may be due to incorrect seam allowances, excessive pressing, stretching, etc. Trimming or extending an edge is a way to compensate so all blocks remain square and equal.

Cut here

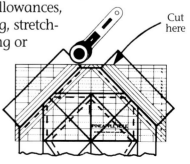

ROUND 4: Cut four 7½″ segments and stitch to block. Press, being careful not to stretch the block. Trim the corners, **lining up the edge of the ruler with the edge of Round 3.**

ROUNDS 5-7: Cut segments (see below) and continue in the same manner as for Round 4.

Round 5 – four 8″ segments

Round 6 – four 9″ segments

Round 7 – four 10″ segments

ROUND 8 (corner): Cut four 7″ segments from the 3″-wide strips in the cutting chart. Stitch to corners of block (corners of block attach to Round 7, center square of block sits on point). Press. Line up one corner of the Pineapple Rule with two adjacent sides of the block. Trim both sides of the corner without moving the ruler.

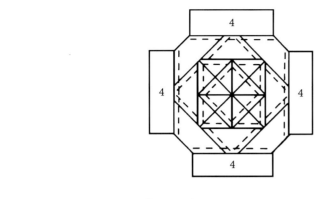

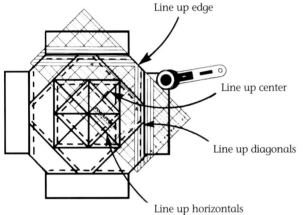

Line up edge

Line up center

Line up diagonals

Line up horizontals

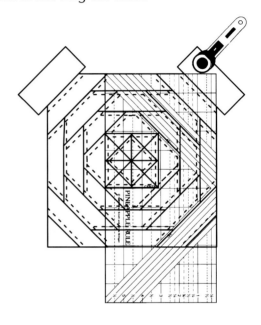

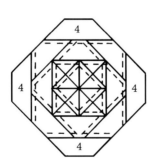

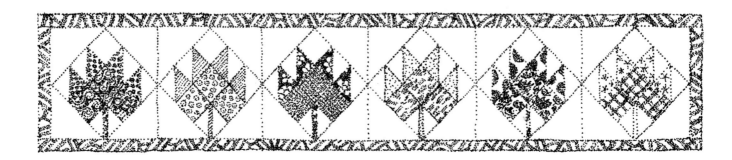

Pineapple Pillowcase

Approximate finished size: 19x29″

Use 42-44″ wide fabric. When strips appear in the cutting list, cut crossgrain strips (selvage to selvage).

Yardage

Scraps (4″ wide & up to 22″ long)	80
	OR 6-8 quarter yards
Binding	⅛ yd.
Backing	1½ yds.
Batting	34x43″

Cutting

Scraps or quarter yards	2 squares – 4″
	70 strips (from 4″ to 22″ long) – 2½″ wide
	8 rectangles – 3x7″
Binding	1 strip – 2½″ wide

Directions

Use ¼″ seam allowance unless otherwise noted.

1. Make two blocks from the directions on pages 38-40. Press well. Stitch one strip to the bottom and three strips to sides of each block. See diagram.
2. Stitch two blocks together as shown. Press.
3. Layer with backing and batting. Quilt as desired. Trim raw edges even with top.
4. Fold pillowcase in half, right sides together, along seam joining blocks. Stitch one short and one long side using a ½″ seam allowance.
5. Bind raw edge.

1.

2.

Home Buddies

Spiced Tea

2 c sugar
2 c orange breakfast drink mix
½ c instant tea
1 pkg. lemonade mix (1 c)
1½ t ground cinnamon
¾ t ground cloves

Mix all ingredients well. Store in covered container. To serve, put 2-3 heaping teaspoons of mix in a cup of hot water. Sit back, put your feet up, and enjoy!

Goose in the Pond

Block Size: 15″ — 12 blocks set with sashing

Approximate finished size: 59x75½″

Use 42-44″ wide fabric. When strips appear in the cutting list, cut crossgrain strips (selvage to selvage). Purchase extra yardage, if necessary, when substituting half-square triangle methods.

Yardage

Background	4⅜ yds.
Dark fabrics	12 quarter yards
Binding	⅝ yd.
Backing	3⅞ yds.
Batting	65x82″

Cutting

Background

For all blocks

Squares	60 squares – 3½″
Half-square triangle units	*72 squares – 3⅞″
Small squares for 9-patches	240 squares – 1½″
Small rectangles	48 rectangles – 1½x3½″
Sashing rectangles	31 rectangles – 2x15½″
Border – large rectangles	14 rect. – 4½x15½″
Border – small rectangles	18 rect. – 2x4½″
Border – corner square	4 squares – 4½x4½″

Darks for 1 block (from each quarter yard)

Half-square triangle units	*6 squares – 3⅞″
Small squares for 9-patches	16 squares – 1½″
Small rectangles	8 rectangles – 1½x3½″
Squares for corners	4 squares – 1¾″
Various darks for sashing	20 squares – 2″
Various darks to finish border	32 squares – 1¾″
Binding	7 strips – 2½″ wide

*Cut these squares in half diagonally to make triangles, or use your favorite method of making half-square triangle units. If using another method, more yardage may be needed.

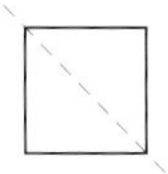

1a. 1b.

Make 12   Add a corner to 4 of the 12

1c. Make 4   1d. Make 4

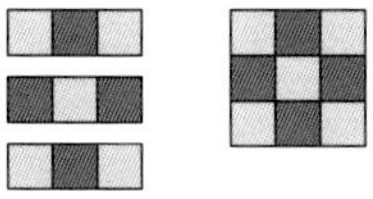

1e.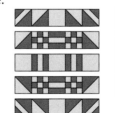

3. 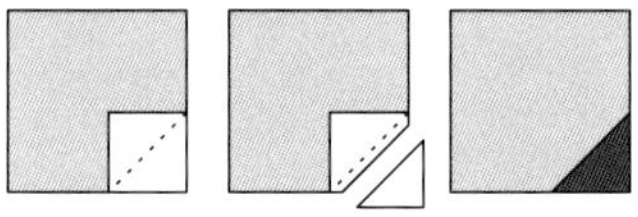 Make 4

4. Make 14

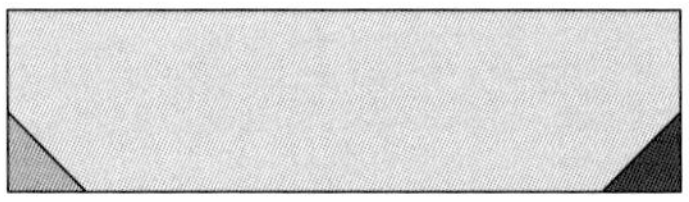

Directions

Use ¼″ seam allowance throughout.

1. For one block:

    a. Make 12 half-square triangle units.

    b. Make four of the above into corner units: Place 1¾″ dark fabric square on light corner of half-square triangle unit, right sides together, mark stitching line with pencil, trim to ¼″ seam allowance.

    c. Make four nine-patch units with the 1½″ squares.

    d. Make four units with the small rectangles.

    e. Finish block using pieced units and five 3½″ squares. See diagram.

2. Make 11 more blocks.

3. Make 4 border corner units with the 4½″ background squares and the 1¾″ dark fabric squares. Use the same method as in Step 1b above.

4. Make 14 border units with the 4½x15½″ rectangles and the 1¾″ dark fabric squares.

5. Make horizontal rows, referring to diagram:

    a. Make top and bottom border rows with border corner units from Step 3, small border rectangles, and large border units from Step 4.

    b. Make three sashing rows with small border rectangles, 2″ dark sashing squares, and 2x15½″ sashing rectangles.

    c. Make four block rows with large border units from Step 4, 2x15½″ sashing rectangles, and blocks.

6. Stitch rows together. Press well.

7. Piece backing horizontally to same size as batting. Use your favorite layering, quilting, and binding methods to finish quilt.

5.

43

Good Ole Summertime

Block Size: 19″ — 12 blocks

Approximate finished size: 57x76″

Use 42-44″ wide fabric. When strips appear in the cutting list, cut crossgrain strips (selvage to selvage).

Yardage

Center square	¼ yd.
Log fabrics	24 quarter yards
Binding	⅝ yd.
Backing	3¾ yds.
Batting	63x82″

Cutting

Centers	12 squares – 3½″
Logs	60-70 strips – 2½″ wide
Binding	7 strips – 2½″ wide

Directions

Use ¼″ seam allowance throughout.

1. Make 12 blocks by stitching strips to center squares in four clockwise rounds. After stitching each strip to block, trim off remaining end of strip. See diagram. Press.

2. Stitch into four rows of three blocks.

3. Stitch rows together. Press well.

4. Piece backing horizontally to same size as batting. Use your favorite layering, quilting, and binding methods to finish quilt.

Round 1

Round 2

Round 3

Round 4

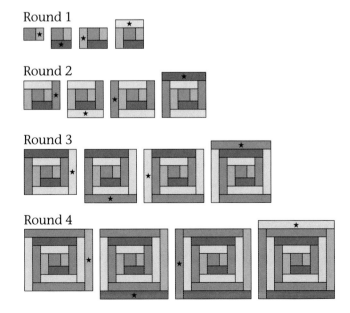

2.

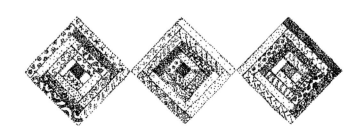

Good Ole Summertime Pillowcase

Approximate finished size: 20x30″

Use 42-44″ wide fabric. When strips appear in the cutting list, cut crossgrain strips (selvage to selvage).

Yardage

Scraps (3½″ wide & up to 24″ long)	48
	OR 6-8 quarter yards
Facing	⅛ yd.
Backing	1½ yds.
Batting	35x46″
Gathered eyelet trim 3-4″ wide	1⅜ yds.

Cutting

Scraps or quarter yards	2 squares – 3½″
46 strips (from 3½″ to 21½″ long) – 2½″ wide	
Facing	1 strip – 2″ wide

Directions

Use ¼″ seam allowance unless otherwise noted.

1. Make two blocks from the directions on page 44. Press well. To each block, add one strip to the bottom and three strips to each side. Cut each strip to length needed before stitching to block to avoid distortion. See diagram.

2. Stitch two blocks together as shown. Press.

3. Layer with backing and batting. Quilt as desired. Trim raw edges even with top.

4. Baste trim to one end of pillowcase, right sides together. Press 2″ facing strip in half wrong sides together. Stitch over trim, raw edges even with bound edge of trim. Fold facing up to cover raw edges and stitch in place by hand.

5. Fold pillowcase in half, right sides together, along seam joining blocks. Stitch end without trim and long side, including trim, using a ½″ seam allowance.

1.

2-4.

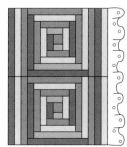

Comfort Quilt

Block Size: 5″ — 140 blocks

Approximate finished size: 50x70″

Use 42-44″ wide fabric. When strips appear in the cutting list, cut crossgrain strips (selvage to selvage).

Yardage

Blocks	20 quarter yards
Binding	⅝ yd.
Backing	3⅜ yds.
Batting	56x76″

Cutting

Block fabrics	7 squares each – 5½″
Binding	7 strips – 2½″ wide

Directions

Use ¼″ seam allowance unless otherwise noted.

1. Arrange squares into fourteen rows of ten squares each.

2. Stitch squares into rows, then stitch rows together. Press.

3. Piece backing horizontally to same size as batting. Use your favorite layering, quilting, and binding methods to finish quilt.

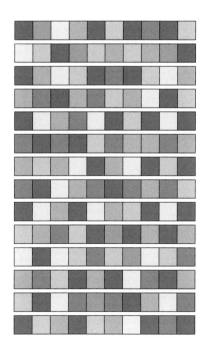

Sweet Lavender

Block Size: 10½″ — 30 blocks

Approximate finished size: 64½x77″

Use 42-44″ wide fabric. When strips appear in the cutting list, cut crossgrain strips (selvage to selvage). Purchase extra yardage, if necessary, when substituting half-square triangle methods.

This antique quilt has sashing seams in different places than we would put them if we were making the quilt, so the diagram and the photo do not match exactly. Directions match diagrams.

Yardage

Background	2⅞ yds.
Medium fabrics (¼ yd. makes 2 blocks)	15 quarter yards
Sashing	2 yds.
Binding	⅔ yd.
Backing	4⅞ yds.
Batting	71x83″

Cutting

Background fabric for all blocks

Half-square triangle units	*60 squares – 4⅜″
Four-patches	240 squares – 1¾″
Corners for four-patches	*240 squares – 2⅝″

Medium fabric for 2 blocks

Half-square triangle units	*4 squares – 4⅜″
Four-patches	16 squares – 1¾″
Centers	2 squares – 4″
Sashing	24 rectangles – 2½x11″
Sashing, border	16 strips – 2½″ wide
Binding	8 strips – 2½″ wide

*Cut these squares in half diagonally to make triangles, or use your favorite method of making half-square triangle units. If using another method, more yardage may be needed.

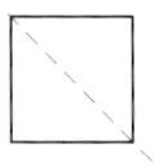

CONTINUED ON PAGE 50

1.

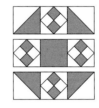

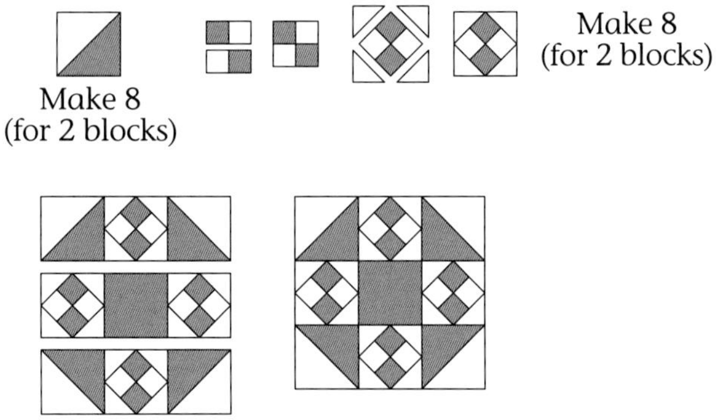

Make 8 (for 2 blocks)

Make 8 (for 2 blocks)

2.

Perennial Pyramids

Unit Size: 6″ tall x 6″ wide

Tablecloth approximate finished size: 48″ square

Quilt approximate finished size: 60x84″

Use 42-44″ wide fabric. When strips appear in the cutting list, cut crossgrain strips (selvage to selvage).

Yardage Tablecloth

Triangle fabrics	136 scraps at least 7″ square or 14 quarter yards
Binding	½ yd.
Backing	3¼ yds.
Batting	52x52″

Yardage Quilt

Triangles	204 scraps at least 7″ square or 21 quarter yards
Border	1¾ yds.
Binding	⅔ yd.
Backing	5¼ yds.
Batting	66x90″

Cutting Tablecloth – Pattern on page 71.

Note: To get ten triangles from each quarter yard, pattern must be rotated.

Triangle fabrics	136 triangles
Binding	6 strips – 2½″ wide

Cutting Quilt – Pattern on page 71.

Note: To get ten triangles from each quarter yard, pattern must be rotated.

Triangle fabrics	204 triangles
Border	8 strips – 6½″ wide
Binding	8 strips – 2½″ wide

Directions

Use ¼″ seam allowance throughout.

1. Tablecloth: Make eight rows of 17 triangles as shown. Quilt: Make 12 rows of 17.

2. Stitch rows together.

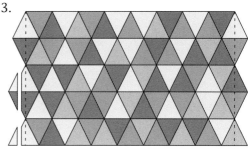

3. Staystitch sides as shown. Trim sides ¼″ outside staystitching.

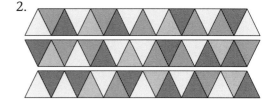

Trim

4. Measure quilt for side borders. Prepare side borders the measured length and stitch to quilt.

Repeat for top and bottom borders. Press well.

5. Piece backing vertically to same size as batting. Use your favorite layering, quilting, and binding methods to finish quilt.

Dresden Plate

Block Size: 15¾" — 20 blocks

Approximate finished size: 74x90"

Use 42-44" wide fabric. When strips appear in the cutting list, cut crossgrain strips (selvage to selvage).

This antique quilt was made whole-cloth, and we adapted it to block construction. Also, the number of border pieces is different in our version.

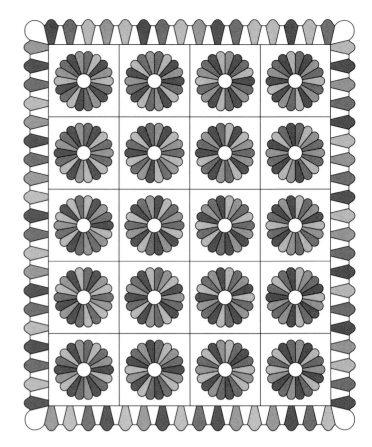

Yardage

Background	6⅜ yds.
Scraps at least 4½x7" to total	8-9 yds.
Binding	1¼ yds.
Backing	5⅝ yds.
Batting	80x96"

Cutting Patterns on pages 66-67.

Background
Blocks	20 squares – 16¼"
Border side – Pattern C	68
Border corner – Pattern D	4
Plate center – Pattern E	20

Scraps
Dresden Plate segments – Pattern A	360
Border – Pattern B	72

Binding   40" square cut into bias strips 2½" wide

Make
20

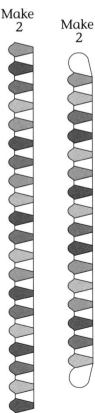

Make
2

Make
2

Directions

Use ¼" seam allowance throughout.

1. Stitch 18 Dresden Plate segments together into a circle. Press seam allowances in a spiral. Applique outside edge to background square. Applique piece E over center of plate. Make 20. Press lightly.

2. Stitch blocks together in five rows of four blocks. Stitch rows together. Press lightly.

3. Border: For sides, stitch 20 B and 19 C together. For top and bottom, stitch 16 B and 15 C together, then stitch D to each end. Adjust to fit quilt by making a few seams between pieces a bit deeper or shallower. Stitch sides to quilt first, then top and bottom.

4. Press border section of quilt well. Piece backing vertically to same size as batting.

5. Use your favorite layering, quilting, and binding methods to finish quilt.

CONTINUED FROM PAGE 46

Sweet Lavender

Directions

Use ¼″ seam allowance throughout.

1. Make two blocks from each quarter yard:

    a. Make 8 half-square triangles units using 4⅜″ triangles.

    b. Make 8 four-patch units using 1¾″ squares.

    c. Stitch 2⅝″ triangles to corners of four-patches.

    d. Finish blocks by stitching units together as shown. Press.

2. Stitch six rows of blocks together with sashing rectangles. Press. Measure width of row and prepare five horizontal sashing strips the measured length. Stitch rows of blocks to rows of sashing. Press.

3. Border: Measure quilt for side borders. Prepare side borders the measured length and stitch to quilt. Repeat for top and bottom borders. Press.

4. Piece backing vertically to same size as batting. Use your favorite layering, quilting, and binding methods to finish quilt.

Housewarming Potpourri

peel from ½ lemon
peel from ½ orange
2 bay leaves
½ c whole cloves
4 small cinnamon sticks
1½ quarts water

Place all ingredients in a small saucepan or potpourri pot. Simmer gently, adding water as needed. Curl up with a good book or get out your most recent quilting project!

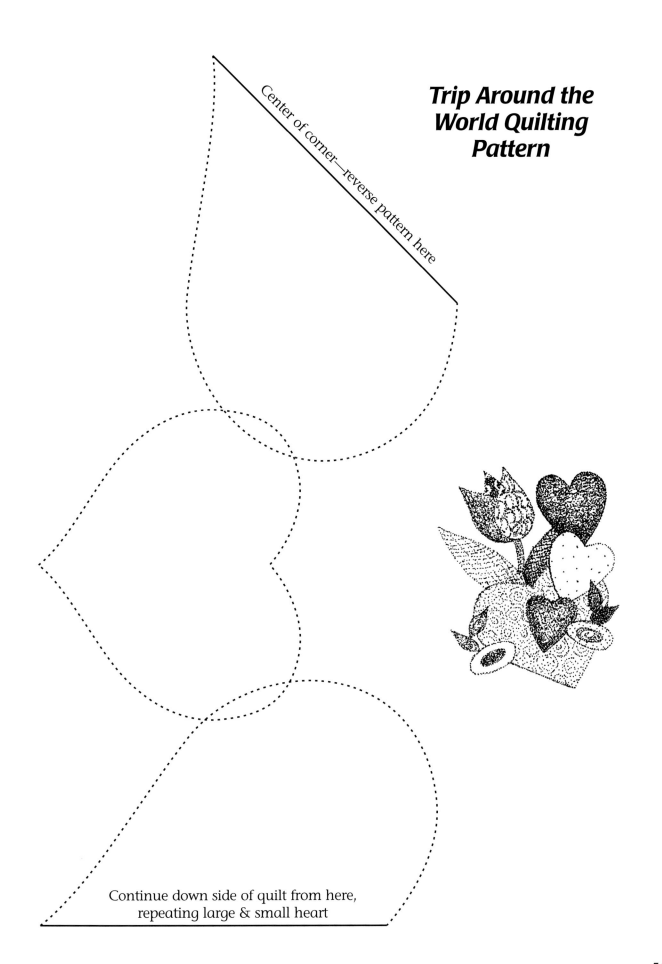

Center of corner—reverse pattern here

Trip Around the World Quilting Pattern

Continue down side of quilt from here,
repeating large & small heart

52 Starry Night

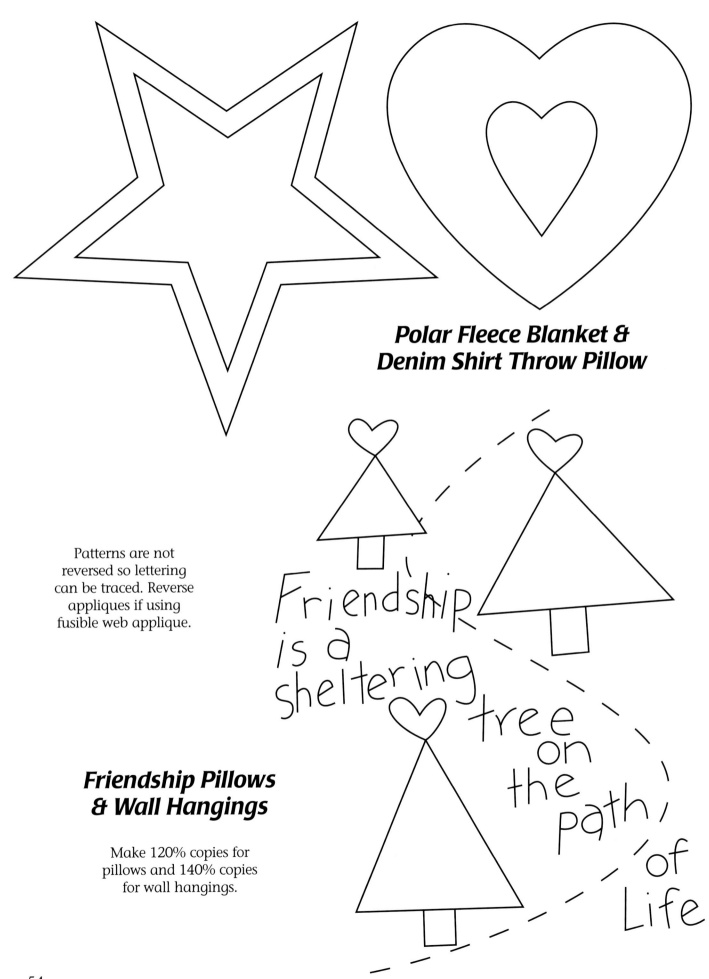

**Polar Fleece Blanket &
Denim Shirt Throw Pillow**

Patterns are not
reversed so lettering
can be traced. Reverse
appliques if using
fusible web applique.

**Friendship Pillows
& Wall Hangings**

Make 120% copies for
pillows and 140% copies
for wall hangings.

Friendship is a sheltering tree on the path of Life

54

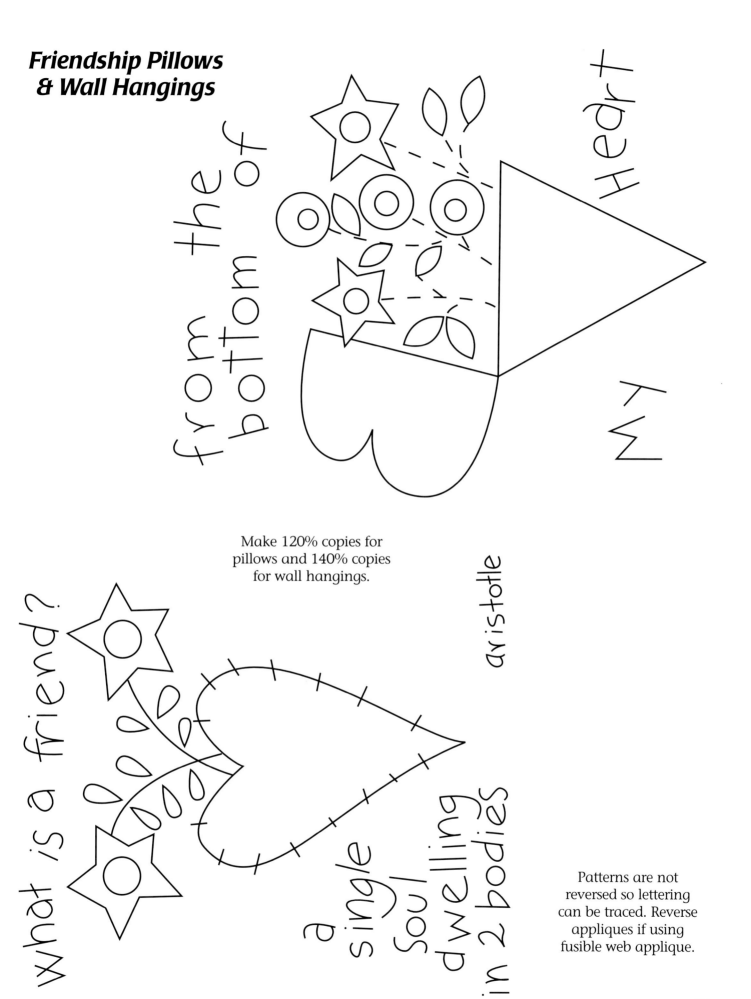

from the bottom of

Heart

My

Make 120% copies for pillows and 140% copies for wall hangings.

aristotle

what is a friend?

a single Soul dwelling in 2 bodies

Patterns are not reversed so lettering can be traced. Reverse appliques if using fusible web applique.

56 Goose in the Pond

Good Ole Summertime & Sweet Lavender   57

Friendship Pillows
& Wall Hangings

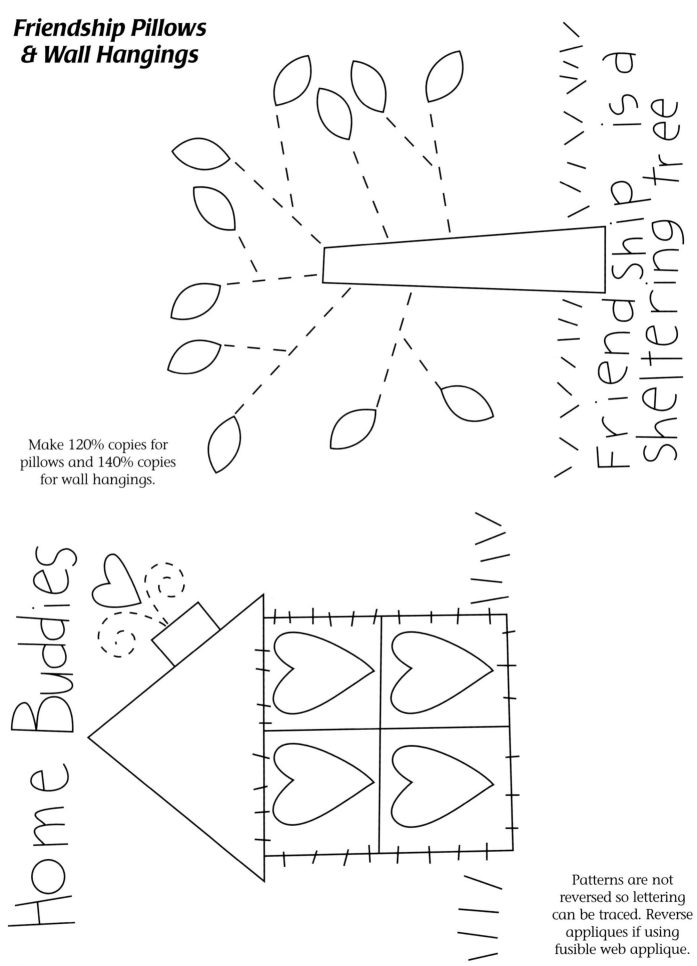

Friendship is a sheltering tree

Make 120% copies for pillows and 140% copies for wall hangings.

Home Buddies

Patterns are not reversed so lettering can be traced. Reverse appliques if using fusible web applique.

Make a 125% copy of
the house/tree pattern
for the chairbacks.

Starry Night Chairbacks, Place Mats, Napkins, & Hot Pad

Patterns are reversed for
fusible web applique; if doing
hand applique, reverse again.

60 Pineapple

Simply Hearts 61

**Garden Wall Hanging
and Chairbacks**

To duplicate our
samples, some of
these patterns
must be reversed
for use in parts of
the design.

62

Garden Wall Hanging and Chairbacks

Garden Chairbacks

Garden Wall Hanging
& Chairbacks

63

64 Perennial Pyramids

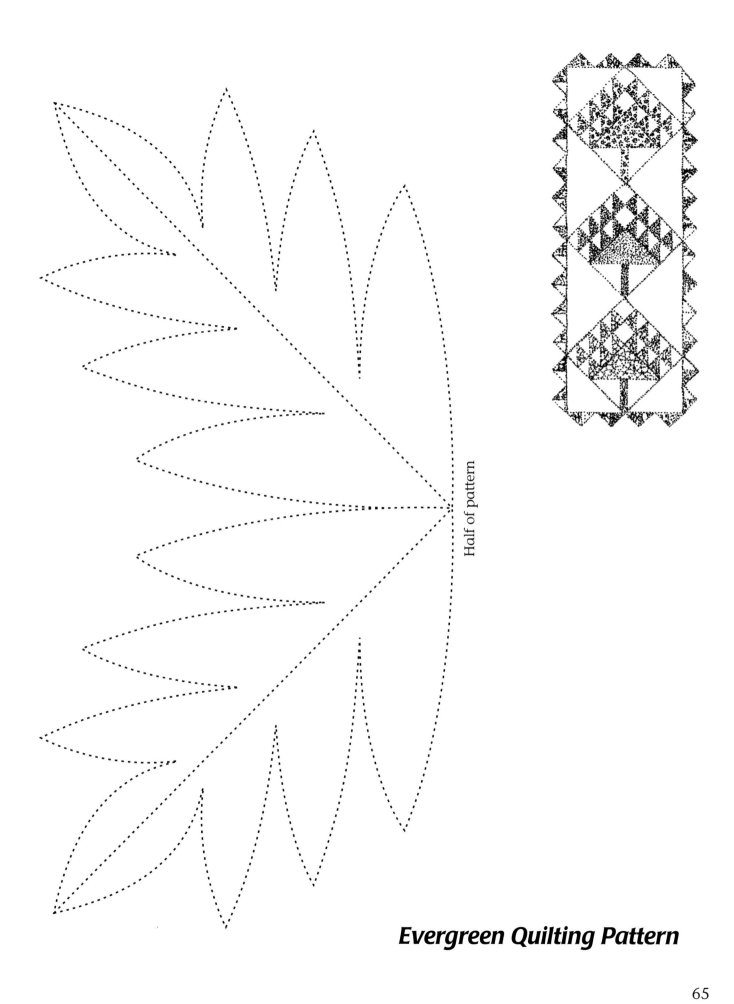

Half of pattern

Evergreen Quilting Pattern

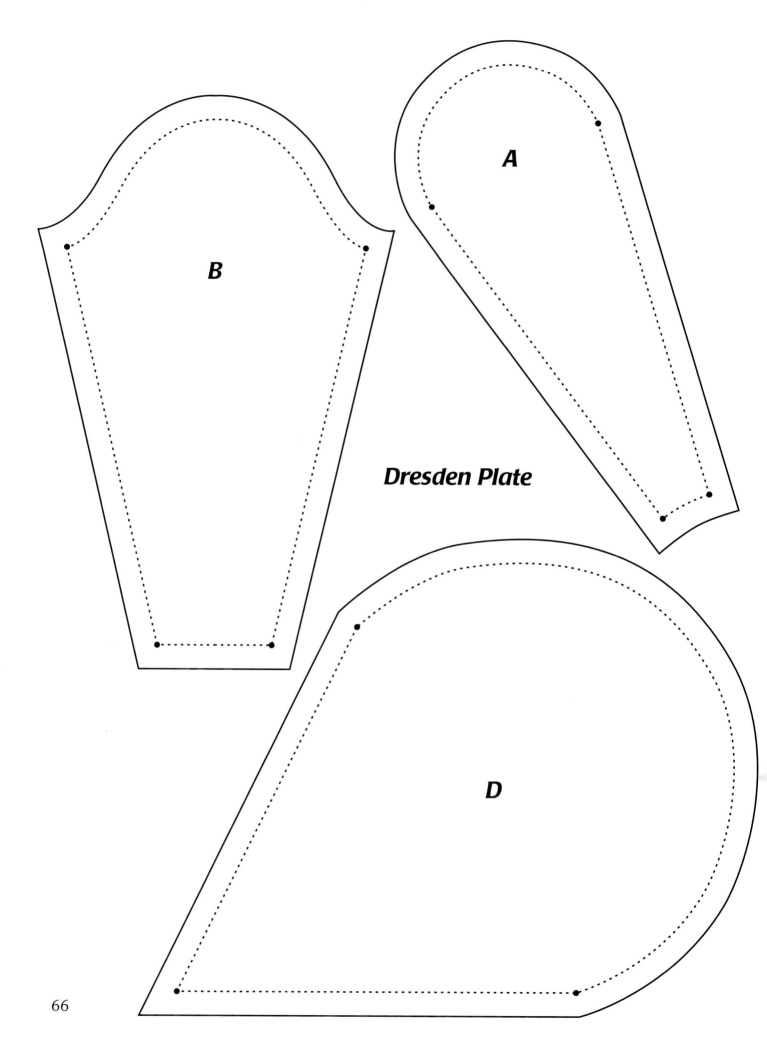

B

A

Dresden Plate

D

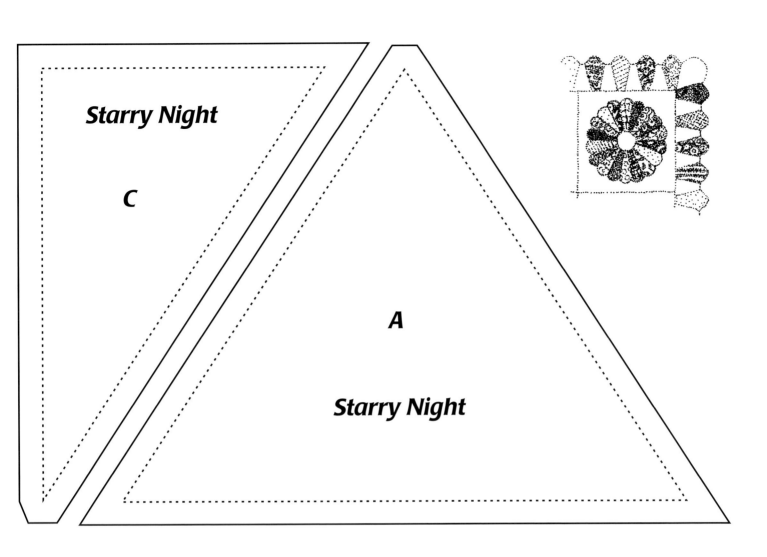

Starry Night

C

A

Starry Night

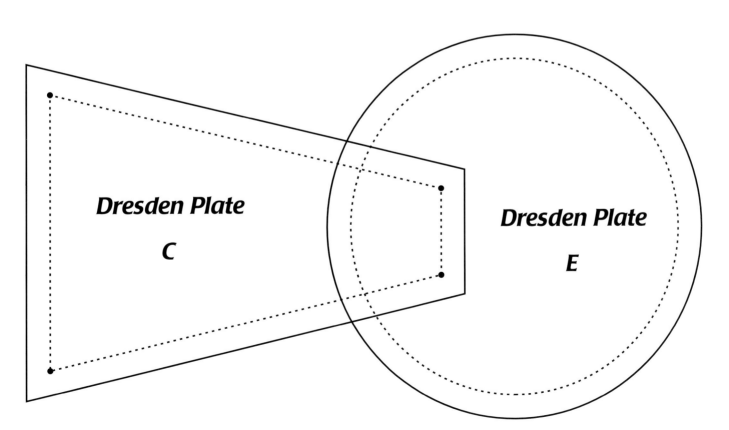

Dresden Plate

C

Dresden Plate

E

Holiday Stepping Stones

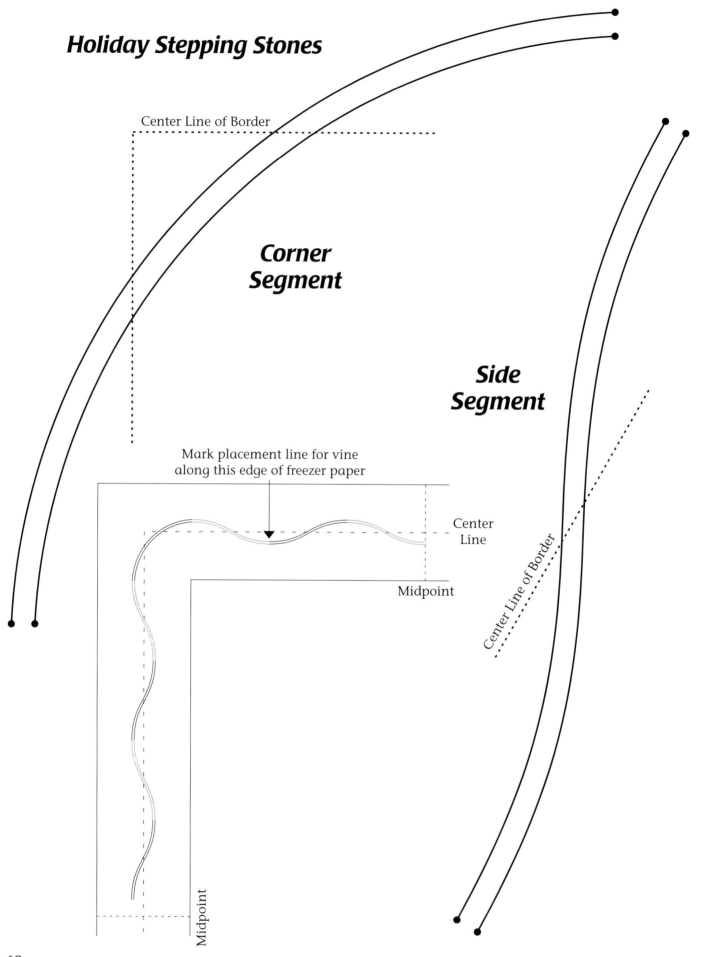

Center Line of Border

*Corner
Segment*

*Side
Segment*

Mark placement line for vine
along this edge of freezer paper

Center
Line

Midpoint

Center Line of Border

Midpoint

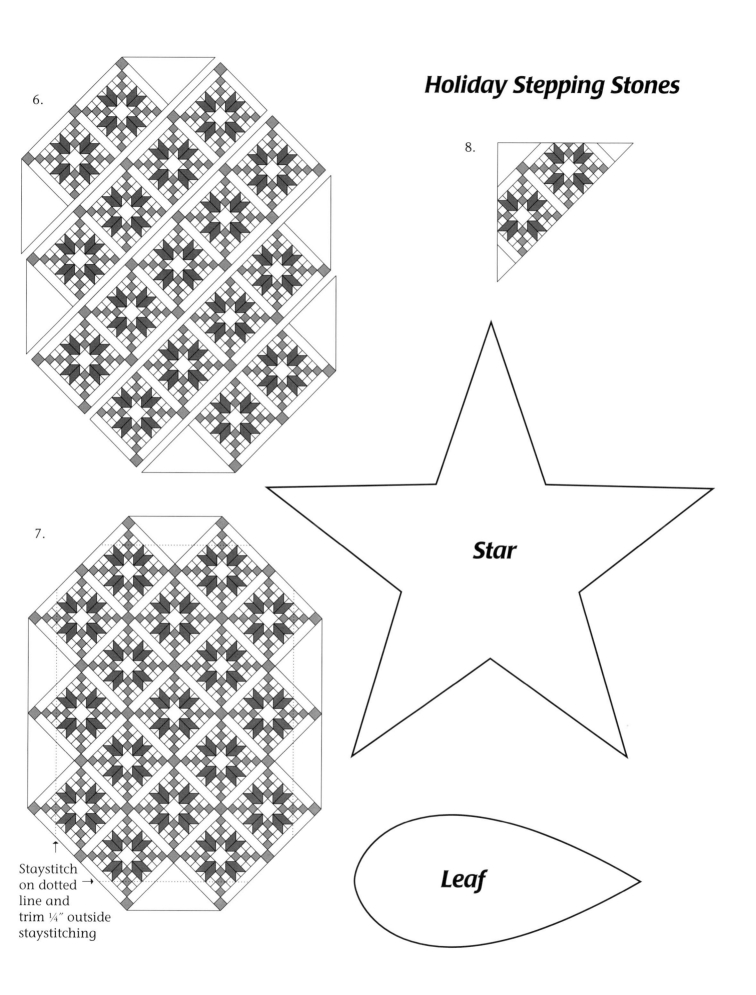

6.

7.

8.

Star

Leaf

↑
Staystitch
on dotted →
line and
trim ¼" outside
staystitching

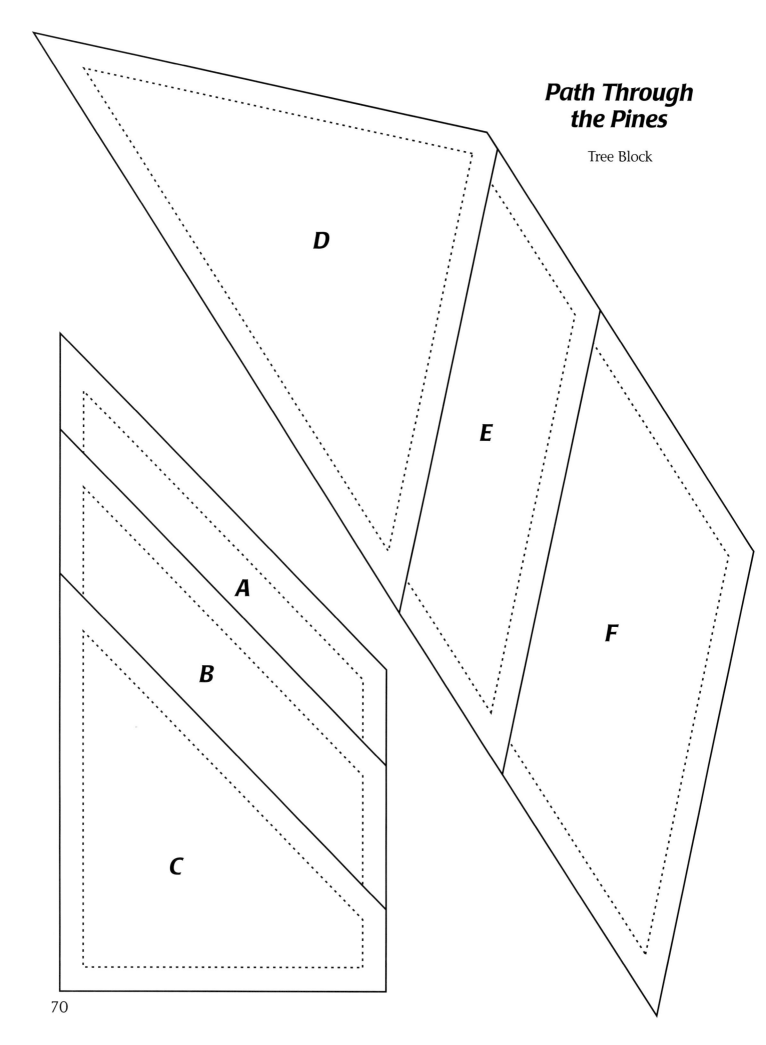

Path Through the Pines

Tree Block

D

E

A

B

C

F

70

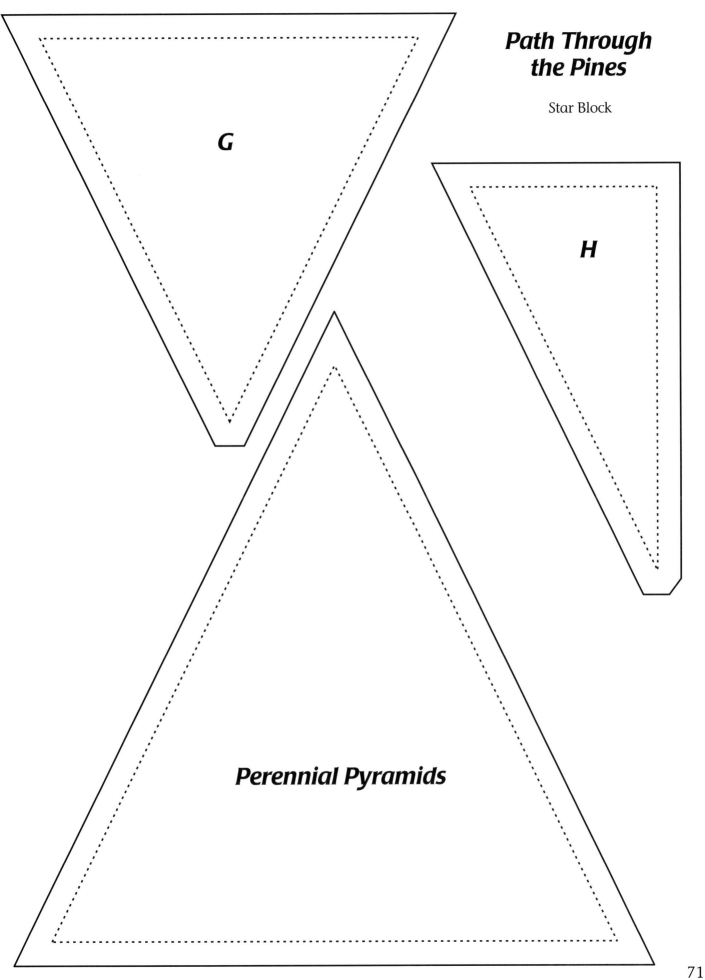

Path Through the Pines

Star Block

G

H

Perennial Pyramids

71

Still Life

Patterns are reversed for
fusible web applique; if doing
hand applique, reverse again.

Patterns are reversed for fusible web applique; if doing hand applique, reverse again.

Still Life

Still Life

Patterns are reversed for
fusible web applique; if doing
hand applique, reverse again.

Still Life

Patterns are reversed for
fusible web applique; if doing
hand applique, reverse again.

Still Life

Patterns are reversed for
fusible web applique; if doing
hand applique, reverse again.

Patterns are reversed for
fusible web applique; if doing
hand applique, reverse again.

Still Life

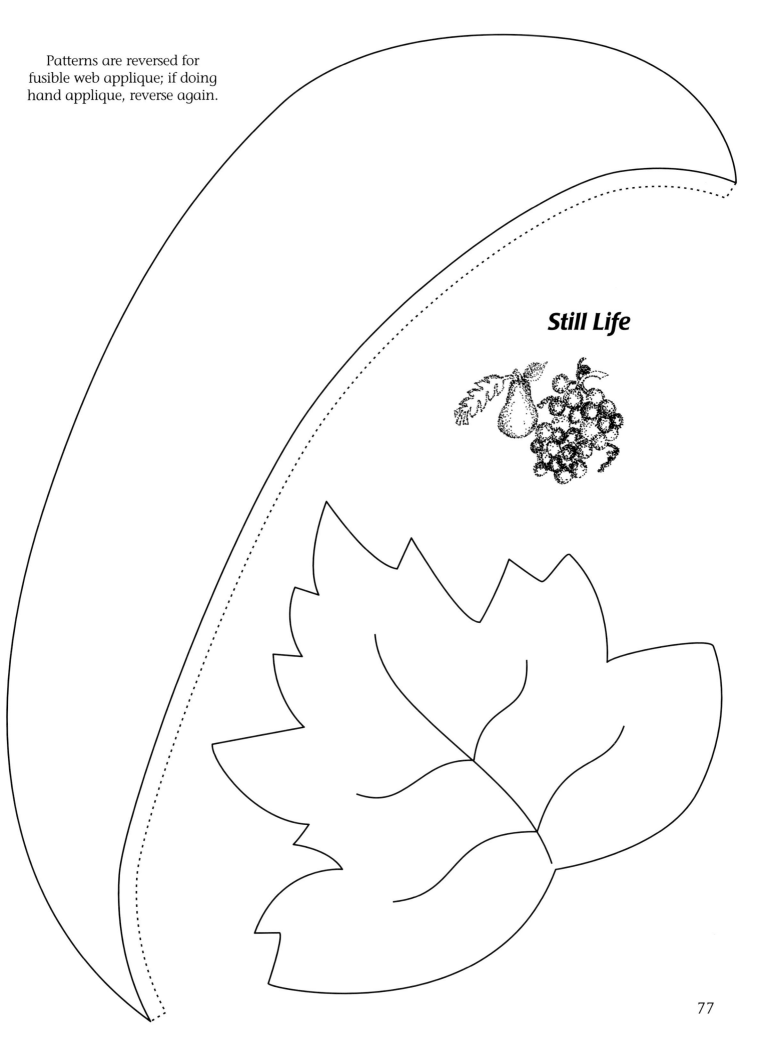

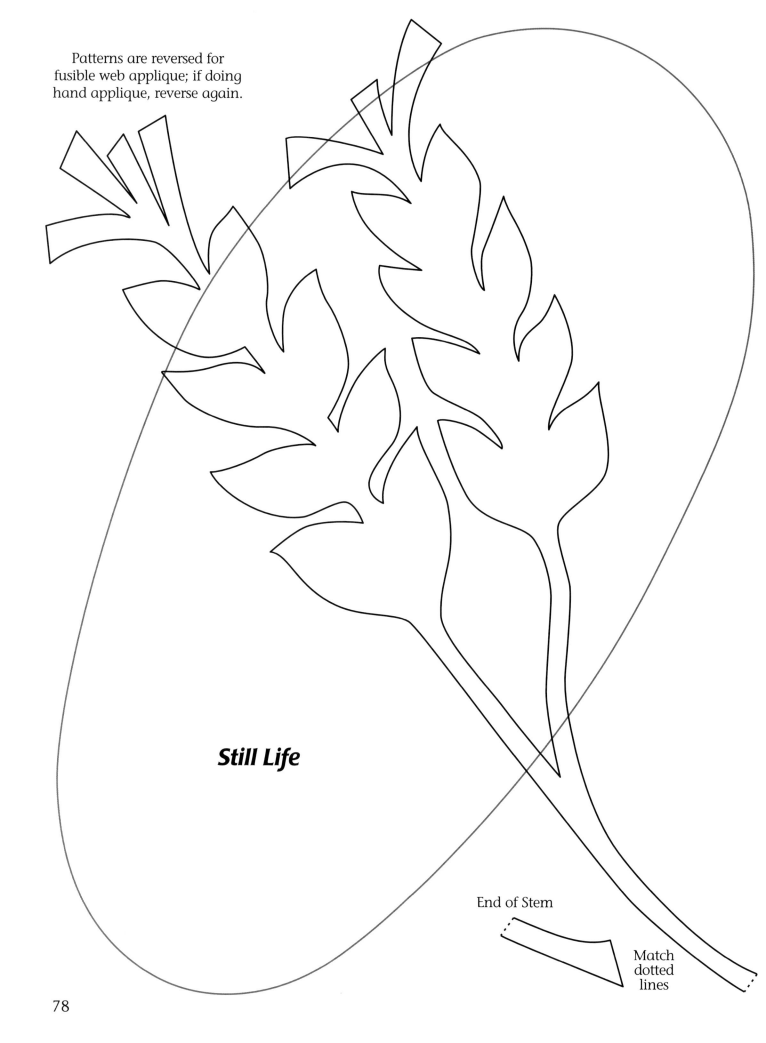

Patterns are reversed for fusible web applique; if doing hand applique, reverse again.

Still Life

End of Stem

Match dotted lines

Still Life

Patterns are reversed for
fusible web applique; if doing
hand applique, reverse again.

79

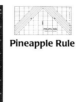